So You Want to Join the

U.S. Peace Corps

Here's the Info You Need

Luke Fegenbush

1405 SW 6th Avenue • Ocala, Florida 34471 • Phone 800-814-1132 • Fax 352-622-1875
Web site: www.atlantic-pub.com • E-mail: sales@atlantic-pub.com
SAN Number: 268-1250

Library of Congress Cataloging-in-Publication Data

Names: Fegenbush, Luke, author.
Title: So you want to join the U.S. Peace Corps : here's the info you need / Luke Fegenbush.
Description: Ocala, Florida : Atlantic Publishing Group, Inc., [2016] | Includes bibliographical references and index.
Identifiers: LCCN 2016047866 (print) | LCCN 2017002318 (ebook) | ISBN 9781620232071 (alk. paper) | ISBN 1620232073 (alk. paper) | ISBN 9781620232088 (ebook)
Subjects: LCSH: Peace Corps (U.S.) | Voluntarism--United States. | Economic assistance, American--Developing countries.
Classification: LCC HC60.5 .F44 2016 (print) | LCC HC60.5 (ebook) | DDC 361.6--dc23
LC record available at https://lccn.loc.gov/2016047866

PROJECT MANAGER AND EDITOR: Rebekah Sack • rsack@atlantic-pub.com
ASSISTANT EDITOR: Yvonne Bertovich • yvonne.bertovich34@gmail.com
INTERIOR LAYOUT: Steven W. Booth • steven@geniusbookcompany.com
COVER DESIGN: Jackie Miller • millerjackiej@gmail.com
JACKET DESIGN: Steven W. Booth • steven@geniusbookcompany.com

Printed in the United States

Reduce. Reuse.
RECYCLE.

A decade ago, Atlantic Publishing signed the Green Press Initiative. These guidelines promote environmentally friendly practices, such as using recycled stock and vegetable-based inks, avoiding waste, choosing energy-efficient resources, and promoting a no-pulping policy. We now use 100-percent recycled stock on all our books. The results: in one year, switching to post-consumer recycled stock saved 24 mature trees, 5,000 gallons of water, the equivalent of the total energy used for one home in a year, and the equivalent of the greenhouse gases from one car driven for a year.

Over the years, we have adopted a number of dogs from rescues and shelters. First there was Bear and after he passed, Ginger and Scout. Now, we have Kira, another rescue. They have brought immense joy and love not just into our lives, but into the lives of all who met them.

We want you to know a portion of the profits of this book will be donated in Bear, Ginger and Scout's memory to local animal shelters, parks, conservation organizations, and other individuals and nonprofit organizations in need of assistance.

– Douglas & Sherri Brown,
President & Vice-President of Atlantic Publishing

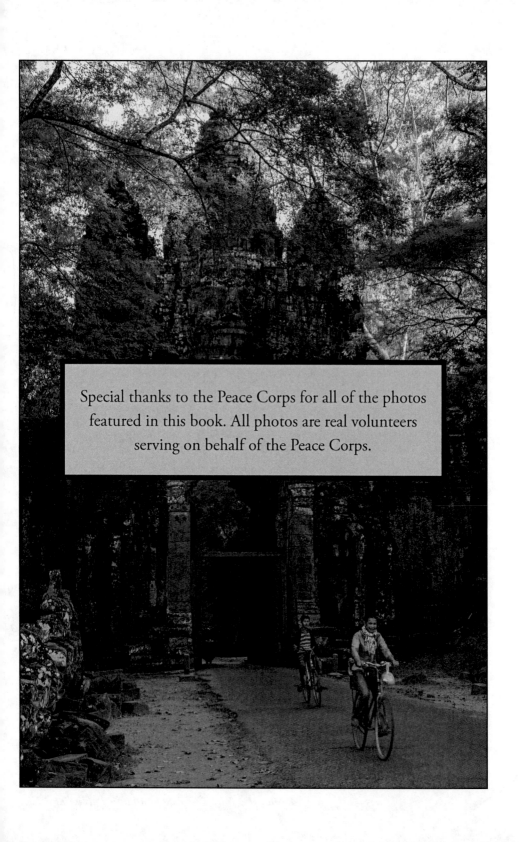

Table of Contents

Chapter 4: What the Peace Corps Asks of Volunteers 57

Chapter 5: Your Actual Chances of Being Hired............................. 61

Introduction

Y ou're in Africa. A few huddled huts and scraggly acacia trees are the only things breaking up a horizon of long, yellow grass. Aside from the huts and the two winding tire tracks that the locals call a road, you brought the only signs of technology with you: a bundle of PVC pipes. It is your job to turn them into a purifier that will provide the thirsty village with disease-free water.

You're teaching English to a classroom of Albanian children. The children travelled narrow goat paths along the foothills to reach the schoolhouse. As they have every morning since they could walk, they started the day with farm chores. In spite of waking up hours before the sun lit the mountaintops, they are alert and eager to learn.

You're in a community that stretches across the savannah and over oceans, ignoring distance and borders and language.

This is the Peace Corps.

Bored, trapped, and in the never-ending hamster wheel of school bus – school – school bus – home, it's easy to feel — in spite of the forced march — that you aren't going anywhere. With the drowning drone of parents and teachers echoing in your head, it's easy to forget that sometimes even good talk doesn't matter if there's not someone listening who will act. It's easy to forget how many people in the world desperately need help and that you can give it to them.

The Peace Corps isn't just an adventure that will let you see places that most people only know exist because of TV. It isn't just an opportunity that will open doors to careers that you've only dreamed of. It's not just a way of helping less fortunate people. It's an experience that will find the best parts of you and make them better. So, buckle up, and let the adventure begin.

Chapter 1
Peace Corps 101

The Peace Corps has more than 50 years of history and a huge range of programs. You don't have to learn everything, but it's helpful to get to know the program to which you may be dedicating years of your life. So, before we get into the roles that you may play as a volunteer, here's a quick overview of the Peace Corps' history, the ideas that its members represent, how its organized, and what the Peace Corps is like today.

How Did the Peace Corps Start?

On October 14th, 1960, soon-to-be president John F. Kennedy arrived at the University of Michigan. It was 2 a.m. He was entering the last three weeks of campaigning, and the long nights and constant travel had exhausted him. But, in spite of the cold, 10,000 students had gathered. They cheered and waved flags and posters decorated with his picture, which had been clipped from the local newspaper.

It was there, at the entrance arch of the Michigan Union, while the rest of the world slept, that Kennedy first shared his idea for a project that would help people no matter where they lived. In those 10,000 students, Kennedy saw a group eager to create a better world. It was the youth of America who would take his words and turn them into action.

Four months later, on March 1, 1961, Kennedy, now president, founded the Peace Corps by executive order. It was a project that realized his ideas of service. As he famously remarked, "And so, my fellow Americans: ask not what your country can do for you — ask what you can do for your country."

Fast Fact *Volunteer safety and security is the Peace Corps' highest priority. The agency devotes significant resources to provide volunteers with the training, support, and information they need to stay healthy and safe.*

The Corps began in Africa, with programs in Ghana and what is now Tanzania. Later that year, the Corps expanded, sending 750 volunteers to 13 countries in Latin America, Africa, South Asia, Asia, and the Caribbean. Early volunteers worked in education, medicine, health care, and community development.

Over the years, the Peace Corps grew. It added business projects in the 1980s. In the 1990s, the Peace Corps expanded into China and countries of the former Soviet Union. Teams of Peace Corps volunteers (PCVs) began offering disaster relief in developing countries. During the new millennium, the Peace Corps expanded its work to include HIV/AIDS education and care. In some countries, Peace Corps programs focused on establishing internet access to remote locations, making communication between volunteers and their loved ones easier than in the past.

Although the Peace Corp has grown, it's not as popular anymore. Since the number of volunteers peaked at more than 15,000 in 1966, it slowed down to a trickle, reaching an all-time low of 5,380 in 1982. Fortunately, the Peace Corps is seeing a resurgence. Its volunteer count now stands at about 7,000, and more are volunteering their skills and time every year.

For a full account of the Peace Corps' history, visit: **www.peacecorps. gov/about/history**.

What is the Peace Corps About?

The Peace Corps' mission is to encourage friendships in other countries by sending Peace Corps volunteers on two-year trips to work, learn, and develop awareness. Even today, the Peace Corps' mission statement has the same three simple goals with which it began (**www.peacecorps.gov/ about**):

1. Help the people of interested countries meet their need for trained men and women.

2. Help promote a better understanding of Americans on the part of the peoples served.

3. Help promote a better understanding of other peoples on the part of Americans.

Although it was founded by the government, the Peace Corps works independently of political interests, providing requested assistance to countries around the world. Since it began, nearly 220,000 Americans have helped communities in over 140 host countries.

How is the Peace Corps Organized?

From Belize to Nepal, the Peace Corps has to cover a lot of ground. To do this effectively, it is organized like the engine of a Prius: efficiently. Its members work together to communicate clearly with government organizations that decide its budgets, host-country governments that dictate what they're allowed to do and where, and volunteers that make it all worth it.

The U.S. government

The Peace Corps is an independent agency within the executive branch of the U.S. government. The President of the United States appoints the Peace Corps director and deputy director, and these appointments are confirmed by the U.S. Senate. Other government agencies help the Peace Corps with its mission. The Senate Committee on Foreign Relations and the House Committee on Foreign Affairs manage the activities and programs of the Peace Corps. The Peace Corps' annual budget is determined each year by the congressional budget and appropriations process.

Head of the Corps

At the top is the director of the Peace Corps. The director speaks to Congress about the needs of the Peace Corps so that they know how much money the budget needs. The director also works with host-country governments and the Secretary of State to make sure that the Peace Corps can accomplish what it needs to do.

Many directors of the Peace Corps, like Carrie Hessler-Radelet and her predecessor Aaron S. Williams, began their career in the Peace Corps as volunteers.

Regional directors

A regional director is responsible for establishing new Peace Corps work sites. A regional director must also develop a relationship with the host-country government, determine the expertise volunteers need at each post, and prepare for the arrival of each team of Peace Corps volunteers.

Regional directors control huge areas. Currently, there are three directors who divide the Peace Corps' sites into three regions. One represents all the countries in Africa. Another works in Europe, the Mediterranean, and Asia. The last represents America and the Pacific.

Country directors

While regional directors work with the big picture, they depend on country directors to work more closely with host countries and their volunteers. The role of each country director is to promote the well-being of volunteers by developing safety policies and making sure staff members are trained to adjust to their new culture. Country directors are also responsible for a budget of up to $4 million per country director. Country directors also work with assistance groups in host countries to establish and plan Peace Corps projects.

Associate Peace Corps Directors

The Associate Peace Corps Director is responsible for selecting and arranging housing for volunteers. The APCD also visits work sites regularly and advises the staff as needed. APCDs provide technical advice and guidance to the country director, they supervise staff in all areas of administrative management, and they are responsible for the following:

- ◊ Budget formulation and execution
- ◊ Human resources
- ◊ Procurement (obtaining supplies)
- ◊ Property
- ◊ Computer systems maintenance
- ◊ General services to the post

They are also responsible for the fiscal integrity of the country program.

The Present-Day Peace Corps

In 2011, the Peace Corps celebrated its 50th anniversary. With this anniversary came a closer examination of the organization's recent shortcomings.

Recently, 20 countries requested PCVs, but there was not enough funding to send new volunteers. In April 2009, President Obama signed the Edward M. Kennedy Serve America Act, which supports expanding the Corps and officially recognizes September 11th as a National Day of Service and Remembrance and encourages all Americans to recommit to service in their communities throughout the year.

Fast Fact

Applications are accepted on a rolling basis. Over the past year, the Peace Corps has received over 15,000 applications, an 18 percent increase over the previous year.

Now is one of the best times to join the Peace Corps. As many of its service areas follow first-world countries into the digital age, it is refocusing to lend aid to a modern world. In no other time have volunteers had access to the training and health and safety resources that they do today. In addition, 92 percent of PCVs have cellphone service and 50 percent have daily access to the internet. It has never been easier to stay in contact while in remote areas.

The Peace Corps has expanded to offer aid to Vietnam and Liberia and hopes to expand the area it serves even more in addition to offering more modern services for a changing world.

The Peace Corps has served 140 host countries to date. Volunteers work with local governments, communities, schools, and entrepreneurs to address needs in education, health, business, information technology, agriculture, youth development, and the environment.

Notable RPCVs

RPCV stands for Returned Peace Corps Volunteer. Here are some names you should recognize if you plan on joining.

◊ Reed Hastings, Netflix founder and CEO taught mathematics in Swaziland from 1983 to 1985

◊ Sen. Christopher Dodd (D – Conn.), served in the Dominican Republic from 1966 to 1968

◊ Mildred Taylor, Newberry Award-winner and author, of *Roll of Thunder, Hear My Cry*, served in Ethiopia from 1965 to 1967

◊ Joe Acaba, mission specialist and educator at NASA, served in the Dominican Republic from 1994 to 1996

◊ MSNBC political commentator Chris Matthews served in Swaziland from 1968 to 1970

◊ Joyce Neu, founding executive director of the Joan B. Kroc Institute of Peace and Justice, served in Senegal from 1972 to1974

◊ Bob Shacochis, American Book Award recipient and author of *Easy in the Island*, served in the Eastern Caribbean from 1975 to 1976

◊ Jim Doyle, governor of Wisconsin, served in Tunisia from 1967 to 1969

◊ Taylor Hackford, Academy Award-winner and producer of the 1982 film *An Officer and a Gentleman* served in Bolivia from 1968 to 1969

◊ This Old House host Bob Vila lent his construction expertise to Panama from 1971 to 1973

◊ Kathy Tierney, vice chair of the board of directors of Sur La Table, served in Fiji from 1967 to 1969

◊ Richard Wiley, winner of the PEN/Faulkner Award and author of Ahmed's Revenge and Soldiers in Hiding, served in Korea from 1967 to 1969

◊ Samuel Gillespie III, senior vice president of Exxon Mobil Corp., served in Kenya from 1967 to 1969

◊ Chyna, professional wrestler and glamour model served in Costa Rica from 1993 to 1995

Case Study

Name: *Richard Lipez*

Assignment: *Education*

Location: *Ethiopia*

Served: *1962–1964*

Post-Eisenhower idealism inspired Richard Lipez to drop out of graduate school and join the Peace Corps. "I was, first of all, caught up in the whole Kennedy-era romance of widening the United States' view of the world," said Lipez, who has a bachelor's degree in English.

Lipez left a small town in Pennsylvania to see a world in which Americans felt more welcome than they do today. In part due to the social climate, Lipez adjusted smoothly to life and work in Africa. Loneliness was not an issue for Lipez because there were approximately 50 other volunteers in the capital (where he taught during his first year of service) and roughly eight other PCVs in the small town where he spent his second year. Ethiopians treated Lipez and his fellow volunteers with kind interest, staring at them in public and exclaiming at the sight of foreigners when they walked by. "It wasn't really that hard to be an object of sort of friendly curiosity," Lipez said.

What frustration Lipez did experience came mostly from coping with political obstacles that stood in the way of his teaching. Pupils in the small school had too few books; so when Lipez and his fellow volunteers found a warehouse full of schoolbooks, they thought the problem had been solved. Their relief was short-lived. The supervisor of the warehouse refused to let them take any books for fear the students would soil or lose them. The department of education would charge the supervisor for the cost of any books that went missing or were returned in less-than-perfect condition. Lipez and his colleagues eventually got official approval to use the books, but not without a trip to the capital and negotiating to ensure that the cost of lost books would not come out of the supervisor's pocket.

The kind of adaptability, patience, and problem-solving Lipez used to get the books released are qualities prospective volunteers should note in their applications. Other traits to emphasize include a deep interest in other cultures and an active imagination.

Openness to cross-cultural friendships and a keen imagination served Lipez well in the Peace Corps and beyond. Lipez counts literary inspiration among the benefits of service. He is the author of a series of mystery novels in which a RPCV is a recurring character. A longstanding bond with members of his host community is another cherished outcome of service. Lipez and his partner recently visited Ethiopia for a reunion with his former students, who held a series of feasts in their honor.

Volunteers leave their host countries with many such intangible rewards for their service. "For ourselves, it was just the most profoundly educating and wonderful experience," Lipez said.

Chapter 2: Peace Corps Perks

"The toughest job you'll ever love."

The millions that were reached by this 1961-1991 ad campaign will recognize this as a slogan for the Peace Corps. But for Peace Corps volunteers, it means something more. It's the reason that they leave everyday conveniences to embark on two-year adventures in developing countries.

There is pay for volunteers (the modest stipend volunteers receive is enough to live in the same conditions as locals, so don't expect to pad your savings account), but few PCVs would say that they joined for the money.

Most applicants, before their assignments, also consider the advantages Peace Corps service gives to those with student debts, to those looking for a job, or for people who just want to see the world. Volunteers who have completed their two-year assignment, however, see it from an entirely different point of view.

The real pay comes in the form of the success of a teacher's students or from the gratitude of an entire community that can now vaccinate their children. The feeling of helping those truly in need, of succeeding in some of the world's most demanding places, cannot be described. It can only be earned.

Help Yourself by Helping Others

Growth is one of the main ways that the Peace Corps rewards its volunteers. As part of their assignments, volunteers constantly learn and adapt to new situations. Adjusting to foreign surroundings makes every day routines anything but ordinary. Through encountering and adapting to foreign circumstances, Peace Corps volunteers grow in self-sufficiency, resourcefulness, and creativity.

Fast Fact Fast Fact: The length of service is 27 months, which includes an average of three months of in-country training and 24 months of volunteer service.

Returned Peace Corps volunteer, Darren Miller, who served in Nepal from 1991 to 1993 found that even something as simple as commuting to work could be an adventure. In the United States he would face crowded subways and jammed highways while going to work. In Nepal, he hiked three hours through a stunning mountain backdrop to get to his work site. Even the familiar smells and sounds of a bus ride were completely gone in Nepal. Rather than dealing with loud cellphone conversations, Miller had the novel experience of riding with the luggage on top of the bus as they negotiated hairpin mountain turns. The seats were too small for long American legs.

Personal growth is not the only benefit of joining the Peace Corps. Volunteers also have the opportunity to alleviate other people's suffering. Volunteers frequently find themselves with a deeper understanding of how people live in poor areas.

Mark Kohn, who served in the Peace Corps from 1979 to 1981 experienced a life-changing event during what might have been a routine visit to the doctor's office. In Micronesia, seeing a doctor requires a three-day boat ride. What would have been a short car ride in the United States became a lifelong memory for Kohn when he witnessed a live birth en route. While living among the natives gave him some idea of how hard life in a remote area could be, this experience changed how he looked at life forever.

Donna Statler, who served in Belize, learned a similar lesson. At dinner with her host family, she was offered a plate of beans. She was about to begin eating when she saw that the rest of the family had no plates. She was told that they expected to have only tea that day. She gave the food back to the children, touched that a family with so little would give what they did have to a stranger.

Volunteers leave the Peace Corps with an expanded understanding of the culture of their country of service. Through two years of becoming acquainted with an unfamiliar country, volunteers grow to look with new eyes at American habits they once took for granted.

Case Study

Heather Windom

Macedonia

Education

I took about a year from application to assignment for my Peace Corps adventure to begin. I had heard that only one out of 10 applicants were chosen, so I was thrilled I was given the chance to go. Letters of reference, essays, and phone interviews accompanied my application — all designed to give the Peace Corps as much information about me as possible.

I was assigned to Macedonia, a former-Yugoslavia country located just above Greece. Before my departure, I received a detailed informational booklet, logistics, and a cultural welcome CD with music and language phrases.

My group landed in Skopje, Macedonia after two flights and a day of traveling. A large bus took us to a town two hours east of Skopje called Kochani. We arrived at a hotel that would be our home for the first week. During that week, we learned the Cyrillic alphabet, met the U.S. Ambassador and the Peace Corps country director, and we got to know one another. At the end of the week, each of our host families came to pick us up.

My host family, Vaska and Aleksandar were charming and set me at ease immediately. Vaska is a kindergarten teacher and Aleksandar, a doctor. Their two children, Maria, 12, and Zoran, 20, quickly became my friends and guides around their town called Vinica.

For the next three months, I spent time learning the language, learning to cook Macedonian cuisine, and immersing myself in the culture. The time with my host family was wonderful and beyond what I had hoped for.

After three months, I was sent to Rostushe, a remote village on the western side of Macedonia, quite a distance from where my host family lived. The Peace Corps pays for each volunteer to have a language tutor if they choose. I found an amazing tutor and friend in the village, and for my first six months there, we worked together for many hours each week. After endless hours of homework, I became about 85 percent fluent in Macedonian. Learning the language was the biggest hurdle, but it was also the key to my success.

For the next two years, I lived the life of a villager high in the Macedonian mountains that bordered Albania. I taught students from 5th to 8th grade about ecology and English. I set up an English club for high school and college students interested in continuing their studies, and I created an English library and media center to promote continued education for children and adults. I helped conduct summer camps for Roma children who learned everything from swimming to lessons about the environment.

I fell in love with the people. I learned about Muslim and Orthodox Christian religions, went to weddings, funerals, and dances, and lived in a 200 year-old stone house that was the perfect sanctuary for me. I made wonderful friends and learned everything I could about the culture, traditions, and history of Yugoslavia. I had the time of my life.

It was in my best interest to have stuck it out through the challenges and occasional doubts. I am a better person for having joined the Peace Corps. I recommend it to anyone who has enough flexibility and open-mindedness to commit themselves to an endeavor beyond their comfort zone. It will be a journey of the heart and soul, one that connects the volunteer to the rest of the world in ways only achieved by true participatory and egoless actions.

College Stuff

Service in the Peace Corps looks good on any application, but you probably weren't counting on the Peace Corps to get you that summer job. (Anyways, fast food restaurants hardly check for a pulse before they throw you in front of a register.) Your biggest worry right now is probably college.

Getting into the Peace Corps without a bachelor's degree is tough, but if you have work experience, you could be a valuable resource for the Peace Corps. You'll also return with a college application that will set you apart from other applicants. Colleges look for applicants who are leaders, who are willing to take risks, and who have a strong sense of social responsibility (**https://bigfuture.collegeboard.org**). These are exactly the traits that the Peace Corps helps its volunteers learn, and when the admissions office sees Peace Corps experience on an application, these are the words that come to mind.

The Peace Corps has had what is called the Master's International program for almost 30 years, but as of September 30, 2016, it has officially come to a close. Don't let that discourage you, though. Having Peace Corps experience is enough to impress anyone taking a look at your résumé.

Help With Student Loan Debt

College price tags get higher every year. Too often, it's considered a given that you'll leave higher education dragging a fat debt behind you. The Peace Corps can help lighten the load. Many colleges and universities offer financial assistance for returned Peace Corps volunteers.

Fast Fact *Competitive applicants demonstrate commitment to community service, leadership experience, and a willingness to learn a new language.*

If you already have student loans and then become a Peace Corps volunteer, you can defer certain loans for up to three years. For federal student loans, this means that while they're deferred, you don't have to pay them. (You'll still have to pay later, but they won't gather the extra interest while they're deferred.)

Other types of loans (Stafford Loans, consolidated loans, and unsubsidized direct loans) will gather interest while deferred, but you still put off paying them. For Perkins loans, 15 percent of the debt can be cancelled out for each of their first two years of service. For the third and fourth year of service, volunteers can cancel 20 percent of the debt.

Those volunteers who have subsidized Stafford Loans can have the federal government pay the interest during the period of deferment.

All of this can be pretty boring, but the bottom line is that you shouldn't let student loans stop you from joining. At the end of your service, you'll be in the same situation as fresh college graduates, except you'll have two years of experience that can't be found anywhere else.

A Résumé That Writes Itself

Although volunteers only receive a small stipend (again, don't expect name brand groceries), joining the Peace Corps is a smart career move that will open career opportunities that are hard to find otherwise.

College graduates who join the Corps gain experience in their field and often serve in positions of greater responsibility than entry-level jobs. You may have heard horror stories about how scarce an entry level experience can be. Peace Corps work experience is a strong answer to the familiar conundrum of needing experience to find a job and needing a job to get experience.

Work experience is only part of what an employer sees when reviewing the résumé of a RPCV. When you have the Peace Corps on your résumé, you draw on the positive reputation of the Peace Corps itself. Add to this the huge network of professionals that volunteers gain when they join the Peace Corps. Fellow Peace Corps volunteers know how valuable the experience is and have access to opportunities all over the world.

In addition, the Peace Corps offers its own job-finding resources through the Office of Returned Volunteer Services. The RVS provides career and education assistance to returned Peace Corps volunteers. The RVS posts jobs for returned Peace Corps volunteers daily at **www.peacecorps.gov/ returned-volunteers/careers/career-link**.

Cushy Government Jobs

Fitted suits. Briefcases. Tax benefits.

Many have looked with jealous eyes at the cushy leather seats of federal employees. If you're among those who hunger for such a position, the Peace Corps can give you the advantage you need. For one year after returning from service, volunteers receive non-competitive eligibility when applying for federal jobs. This means that returned Peace Corps volunteers receive job offers directly, without the position being announced to other applicants. Returning volunteers need only meet the minimum qualifications of the job descriptions. With non-competitive eligibility, returned volunteers are considered federal employees and can apply for jobs that are usually filled by people who already have a government job. This means beginning at a higher level of pay. The two years of service also count towards retirement benefits and vacation time.

# Chapter 3: Where Do You Fit In?

Whether you've already decided to join the Peace Corps or you're just considering it as an option, it's helpful to pick a field that you're interested in and a country that needs help in that area. This could be something that you've had experience in and liked or something that you want to work towards. You might not be ready to get on a plane tomorrow, but there are opportunities all around you that will prepare you for future Peace Corps service. These experiences will help you decide where you fit in.

Where Can You Go?

Take a breath. If you're not seated, do so now. The range of places where Peace Corps volunteers travel is staggering. Many go glass-eyed at the mere sight of a globe, their minds wandering through primeval forests and arctic plains. Because you've read this far, we can only assume that you are especially susceptible.

After a minute (perhaps several) of indulging your travel fantasies, go find a mirror. Look yourself sternly in the eyes. Now tell yourself that they are just fantasies. Break it to yourself easy; you're sensitive.

The needs of the Peace Corps are ever-changing. Applicants are sent where they are needed first, and their requested countries are considered afterward. So try not to set all your hopes on one location. You can always refuse to go to a country, but it's better to examine the reasons you want to volunteer now. It's better than finding out after you've put all the work into crafting your application that what you were really looking for was a vacation.

So keep your passion for exploration, but keep it on a leash. Stay excited, but also stay grounded. Expect the unexpected, but know that it will still surprise you.

For specific information on the regions in which the Peace Corps operates, visit their interactive map at **www.peacecorps.gov/countries**.

Fast Fact — The application process to join the Peace Corps averages 9-12 months.

Africa

To someone living in a first-world country, the cultural idea of Africa is immediate. Already, visions of gazelle and giraffes are prancing through your head. Perhaps tribal villages with sad and hungry children followed these images. These places do exist, but Africa is a huge continent, and its needs are more diverse than popular culture would have you believe. Volunteers are just as likely to be assigned to cities as to outlying villages.

Africa is the Peace Corps' busiest continent, containing 27 countries of service. Volunteers assist with health needs, business development, and education, so if you have experience in any of these areas or are planning on studying them, this region might be a good fit.

Official languages include Zulu, French, Arabic, English, and many local languages. Many countries of service are former colonies that have become republics; some have figurehead monarchies.

The Caribbean

The Caribbean is typically thought of as a paradise, and, to American tourists, it may be. But the reality of living in the Caribbean is far different. The Caribbean countries that the Peace Corps currently serves (Dominican Republic, Eastern Caribbean, and Jamaica) are plagued with natural disasters, shortcomings in education, and poverty. Volunteers are needed for community economic development, education, environment, health, and youth in development.

The climate of the Caribbean is tropical and varies by elevation. At sea level, it stays hot and humid year round, with temperatures ranging from the 70s to the 90s (in degrees Fahrenheit), so if tank tops and sandals aren't your style, you might consider requesting a different country.

Most residents are Christian, but a minority is Rastafarian. Inhabitants speak Spanish, English, French, Dutch, Haitian Creole, and Papiamento along with regional creoles (languages that grew from the simplified dialects that people with no common tongue used) and dialects. Volunteers can expect to learn Spanish and Haitian Creole in the Dominican Republic and Jamaican Patois in Jamaica. In the Eastern Caribbean, languages are much more diverse and include many localized dialects.

Eastern Europe and Central Asia

Mountain ranges and seas make this region especially diverse. Its climate ranges from temperate to semi-arid. Geographic features include beaches, steppes, deserts, and plains. The region includes former Soviet states and a former Yugoslav state. Earthquakes, droughts, and tsunamis are among the natural hazards.

The languages of Eastern Europe and Central Asia are as diverse as its climate. Inhabitants speak Russian, Greek, Gagauz, and Lezgi. Residents are Muslims, Christians, and followers of the Yezidi religion.

Most of the nine countries included are in need of education as well as community economic development.

Asia

There are nine countries of service in Asia, ranging from rural to urban environments. Most countries have Peace Corps projects in education. Other projects include agricultural work in Nepal and community economic development in Timor-Leste.

The climate ranges from tropical and subtropical to desert and continental. Monsoons are regular occurrences in coastal areas, making preparation and rebuilding efforts a necessity. Countries are governed by the National Assembly, members of the Communist party, and monarchs.

Languages spoken include: Mandarin, Spanish, Khmer, French, Russian, Turkic, Khalkha Mongol, English, Filipino, Tagalog, and Thai. Inhabitants are Buddhist, Muslim, Christian, Shamanist, and atheist.

Central America and Mexico

The Peace Corps serves seven countries in Central America and Mexico. Projects vary, but many of the countries need help in both health and economic development. Countries like Mexico and Panama have environmental concerns. Panama also needs help with agriculture.

The climate ranges from tropical to subtropical to temperate to cool. Terrain includes swamps, plains, mountains, and volcanoes. Countries of service are democracies and republics.

Languages spoken include: English, Spanish, Creole, Garifuna, German, Quiche, Kelchi, Nahuatl, and Miskito. Most residents follow Christianity or adhere to indigenous faiths.

North Africa and the Middle East

This region contains only Jordan, Tunisia, and Morocco. It would be faster to refer to the region as "Jordan, Tunisia, and Morocco," but they keep the current name in case they want to add more countries later, plus there are many countries that were served in the past, such as Iran, Libya, and Yemen, to name a few. Efforts here focus on youth development. This means engaging young people in constructive projects, like technology and health education, that will help them lead healthy, successful lives.

Residents speak Arabic, English, and (in Morocco) Berber.

Jordan is a constitutional monarchy. Its people follow Christianity, Islam, and the Druze religion. Tunisia is a democracy. It is dominantly Muslim with Christian and Judaic minorities.

Pacific Islands

The Pacific Islands include small, scattered groups of islands east of Australia, as close to the United States as Samoa. The following islands are currently being served: Fiji, Micronesia, Samoa, Tonga, and Vanuatu.

The cultures of the Pacific Islands are diverse. Volunteers can expect to learn local languages. English is spoken everywhere, but other local languages include Bislama, Tongan, Samoan, Fijian, and Palauan. World languages such as Hindi and French are also spoken. Religions include: Christianity, Islam, Hinduism, Baha'i, and Modekngei. Political systems include constitutional governments and parliamentary democracies.

Health and education are huge issues in the Pacific Islands and most volunteers here can expect to work in one of the two areas.

The climate is tropical; typhoons and cyclones are among some of the natural dangers. Features of the terrain include mountains, plains, desert, plateaus, and volcanoes.

South America

In the five countries of service in South America, health, education, and youth development are the most pressing projects. Volunteers can expect to teach or work on medical projects.

Inhabitants speak English and Spanish as well as more localized languages such as Creolese, Quechua, Kichwa, and Guarani.

South America's climate is mostly tropical, with high temperatures and heavy rainfalls. There are exceptions, like the Atacama desert in Chile, which is one of the driest places on Earth.

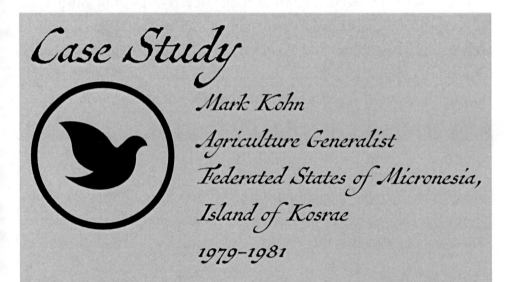

Case Study

Mark Kohn
Agriculture Generalist
Federated States of Micronesia,
Island of Kosrae
1979–1981

Realistic expectations are key to a fulfilling experience in the Peace Corps. Volunteers should respect the knowledge that people in their countries of service have, and not join expecting to change the world. PCVs should also keep in mind that they might not "see the world," as such, but helping to improve the lives of small groups of people and getting to know a corner of the world, to which they might not otherwise have traveled, makes time in the Peace Corps a valuable experience. "I got to experience and see things I only dreamed about. I actually, in small, hard-to-fathom ways, made a difference in another culture," Kohn said.

Just as realistic expectations are essential to succeeding as a volunteer, so is flexibility. Applicants should be willing to go anywhere and do any job.

Remaining flexible regarding locations and assignments helped Kohn secure an invitation to join the Peace Corps in spite of competing with applicants who had more-advanced degrees. Kohn had an associate's degree and had worked as a mailman and an assistant manager of a book shop. Working with senior citizens as a VISTA volunteer and a lifelong interest in overseas service prompted Kohn to apply to the Peace Corps.

Spending two years in a location that had no telephone service, where the wait between available airline flights was measured in weeks, meant that isolation was a problem. Kohn began his service with two other PCVs, but they left the island early. The residents were extremely attentive, going out of their way to keep Kohn company, even if they did not know him. But language and cultural barriers still caused him to feel isolated. Over time, Kohn began to immerse himself in the language. He learned the skills needed for his work and personal life. Kohn left the Peace Corps more focused, self-sufficient, and ready to start the next chapter of his emotional and professional life.

Kohn credits the Peace Corp with giving him the resourcefulness and self-confidence to succeed in his career as a social worker with the Wisconsin Department of Corrections. RPCVs should use examples from their service to convince prospective employers that they are committed and flexible. "When being interviewed for post-Peace Corps jobs, be sure to stress the aspect of all the hardships you experienced and all the moments you had to 'think on your feet.' Employers like to know their staff can handle whatever comes their way," Kohn said.

What Can You Do?

Deciding to join the Peace Corps is a big decision, but it is not the toughest decision future volunteers have to make. A good application will play to your strengths, so it's important to know what you can offer and where it's needed before you start. Have you worked on a farm? The Peace Corps has a variety of agricultural efforts where that experience would go to good use. Maybe you've volunteered as a tutor. This could be applied to education projects.

Fast Fact The minimum age for Peace Corps service is 18; there is no upper age limit.

Some projects can be as intricate as establishing computer labs with internet access to a simple task of building containers for clean drinking water. The focus of Peace Corps projects varies from region to region. Peace Corps volunteers in areas with a high incidence of HIV infection participate in AIDS prevention outreach regardless of their field of expertise. In regions with precarious food supplies, all volunteers address food security issues.

When you consider the area that you want serve in, keep in mind that you'll be devoting two years of your life to it. If it's something you're passionate about, you'll not only be a valuable asset, but your time in the Peace Corps will be more enjoyable and more meaningful.

More information on different fields can be found on the Peace Corps website at: **www.peacecorps.gov/volunteer/what-volunteers-do**.

Education

If you enjoy sounding smart or like kids, this might be the service area for you. Those who already have teaching experience will have the refreshing experience of a more grateful classroom. (Don't set your hopes too high, though; snotty kids are universal.)

Education is the most popular Peace Corps service area; 37 percent of volunteers are involved in some sort of teaching. Future Peace Corps educators will want a combination of college study and teaching experience. Most education positions begin in May/June. All positions require at least a bachelor's degree and a minimum GPA of 2.5.

The following are sub-fields within the education service area:

Elementary education

Teachers of elementary school kids should have a bachelor's degree in elementary or early childhood education. A teaching certificate is not required, and applicants can qualify with a bachelor's degree in other fields or by drawing on their experience working with young children or developing curriculums. Other teaching experience could include work as a substitute or as a teacher in early childhood programs or elementary schools.

Volunteers help native teachers with professional development, instructional methods, and occasional class instructions. Volunteers in elementary education specialize in a particular segment of the sector such as child psychology, English instruction, teaching a language other than English, science, AIDS prevention, or remedial classes.

Secondary education

Volunteers who qualify to train secondary English teachers must have at least a bachelor's degree in education, English, English as a second language (ESL), or a foreign language. A tolerance for pubescent youth is also a must. A master's degree in ESL instruction, applied linguistics, or foreign language can improve an applicant's chances. Applicants don't have to be certified to teach, but experience as a student teacher, teacher's assistant, or substitute is a definite plus.

University instructors

This one probably isn't in your near future, but if you like to plan ahead, and those plans involve a master's degree in English with a concentration in writing, literature, rhetoric, or speech, you might be an ideal candidate for teaching college level classes in the Peace Corps.

Volunteers with a master's degree in a language other than English or who have taught English as a second language, linguistics, or other fields in the humanities improve their chances of acceptance. Other teaching experience should include work as a teacher's assistant, substitute, or tutor. Experience working on student publications or as an adult literacy tutor is a plus.

Volunteers who work at the university level collaborate with other teachers and teach classes in all aspects of languages.

Special education

Volunteers who qualify to work in special education must have a bachelor's degree in education and certificates qualifying them to teach students with special needs. Applicants who have experience working with people with physical, emotional, learning, or developmental disabilities, or those who have experience with people with visual and auditory impairments may qualify. Experience working on the staff of a group home, or having been a volunteer with the Special Olympics, is a plus.

Volunteers who work in special education provide resources for instructors of students with disabilities and advise them on classroom management.

Mathematics

Volunteers who want to teach math need a bachelor's degree in mathematics, computer science, or engineering. Volunteers who minored in mathematics and those certified to teach mathematics at the secondary level but have degrees in unrelated fields might also qualify.

Science

Volunteers who seek science teaching assignments must have a bachelor's degree in general science, biology, chemistry, physics, or engineering. Volunteers with a degree in secondary education with a concentration in science may qualify. Those who have degrees in any field with certification in secondary science may also qualify. Applicants should have experience teaching and tutoring small groups or have volunteer experience with youth programs.

English

Volunteers who wish to teach secondary English can have a bachelor's degree in any field, but they need experience teaching or tutoring English or English as a second language. Volunteers should also have experience with youth-oriented community organizations or have worked in daycare centers.

Volunteers who teach English at the secondary level must conduct conversational classes, teach English as a second language, instruct students in English as it relates to other subjects, and develop curriculum material with other teachers.

Fast *Fact* *Peace Corps volunteers must be U.S. citizens.*

Youth Development

PCVs who work in youth development are responsible for establishing community projects to help children, teens, and young adults who are likely to drop out of school, become unemployed, or contract HIV. Five percent of volunteers work in the youth development sector.

Volunteers who qualify for youth outreach should have at least three month's experience working in youth services, six months working full-time with youth (preferably in a city), or should have experience as physical educators. Volunteers with experience in conflict resolution, AIDS education, fundraising, or helping young people with disabilities is a plus.

Community Development

Community development means working with the individuals of a community to find out what they need and making sure they get it. Successful applicants can have a bachelor's degree in any discipline, but a degree in psychology with a focus in counseling, community development, or social work is a plus. PCVs must have recent experience in counseling, organizing, or leadership. Experience in adult education or assessing community needs is a plus.

Environmental Education

Have you ever subscribed to text updates concerning rainforest deforestation? Do you have handcuffs for the sole purpose of chaining yourself to logging sites? Do you have trouble keeping your sweaters free from bark? Maybe you don't hug trees, but your love and concern for the earth is no less sincere (if a little more subdued). In either case, you might be happy working to promote recycling and conservation of trees and wildlife in service countries. Environmental education involves teaching youth of all ages about conservation and setting up environmental organizations and sanitation programs in cities. Fourteen percent of volunteers work in the environmental sector.

Successful applicants must have a strong science background and a bachelor's degree in ecology, environmental science, or natural-resource conservation. Volunteers with related work or volunteer experience can compensate for a degree in a non-environmental field. PCVs should have work experience in organizing conservation projects, grant writing, teaching, and camp counseling.

Conservation and Park Management

This is another one for the environmentally minded. Volunteers who work in conservation and park management train park rangers, assist with wildlife counts, and promote sustainable harvesting of resources.

Successful applicants must have a bachelor's degree in management of wildlife, natural resources, recreation, or park administration. Peace Corps volunteers should have worked at parks, zoos, or museums; other work experience includes taking flora and fauna inventories, grant writing, or participation in tree-planting efforts.

Environmental Engineering

PCVs who work in environmental engineering concentrate on water utilities and waste management.

Applicants must have at least a bachelor's degree in environmental or civil engineering. Volunteers without a college degree may qualify if they are certified to handle hazardous materials or to operate water treatment plants.

PCVs who are in outstanding physical condition are considered strong candidates. They are also favored for acceptance as Peace Corps volunteers, along with those who have a knowledge of bookkeeping and a background in construction or public health.

Business

Business volunteers address problems such as joblessness, overpopulation, and poorly-trained employees. Some PCVs act as leaders to help the economy by guiding businesses, municipal governments, schools, and community organizations. Volunteers share expertise in financial planning, business design, product development, and marketing. Fifteen percent of volunteers work in the business sector.

Applicants with a variety of educational backgrounds qualify. Successful applicants must have a bachelor's degree in business or related fields. Experience in accounting, running small businesses, cooperatives, or credit unions could compensate for a bachelor's degree in non-business fields.

Volunteers without a degree should have at least four years experience managing a business. Those who have owned or managed a small business are considered strong candidates. Successful applicants will demonstrate multi-tasking skills. Popular backgrounds for applicants include human resources, marketing research, fundraising, and agriculture.

The following are subfields within the Peace Corps' business service area:

Business development

Volunteers who work in business development teach in technical schools, high schools, universities, community organizations, and institutes. PCVs also design curriculum materials, help increase the financial power of women and minorities, and assist with government plans for economic growth.

Successful applicants must have a MBA or master's degree in public administration, management, accounting, banking, or finance with two years of related work experience. Applicants with a bachelor's degree and five years of related work experience may qualify.

Successful applicants for positions in business development have at least two years of related experience and experience as the owner and operator of their own business. Volunteers will be familiar with different management philosophies, have relevant computer skills, and experience developing budgets.

Those applicants who work in development of non-governmental organizations make spending plans, business strategy plans, and mission statements. PCVs are also responsible for recruiting and training volunteers.

Civil planning

Some business volunteers will devote their time to planning at the city and regional levels. These PCVs are responsible for impact assessment (thinking about the consequences of business plans), budget planning, and communicating between government organizations and communities.

Successful applicants must have at least a bachelor's degree in planning, public administration, or public policy. Applicants with a bachelor's degree in architecture or related fields and at least a year of work in planning may qualify. Other volunteers with a bachelor's degree in unrelated fields, five years of related work experience, and three years of employment in planning may also qualify. Some applicants will have experience working with service groups or planning commissions.

Agriculture

Agricultural volunteers help farmers provide balanced diets and establish food security within communities. They also help farm families become financially self-sufficient and learn how to conserve natural resources. PCVs also assist farmers with business procedures such as analyzing profitability of crops and forming associations between farm businesses. Six percent of volunteers work in the agriculture sector.

The following are sub-fields within the Peace Corps' agriculture service area:

Agriforestry

Volunteers who work in agriforestry are not required to have a college degree, but they must have one year of related experience. Successful applicants will have worked at least three months in gardening, landscaping, planting trees, managing livestock, or raising fish and should have a familiarity with environmental issues. Tutoring experience is helpful.

Applied agriculture

PCVs who work in applied agriculture promote organic growing, farm management, and teach agricultural methods. Volunteers encourage composting and organic methods to repel vermin.

Successful applied-agriculture applicants must have a bachelor's degree in agricultural science. Those without a degree must have three years' experience farming full-time. Applicants who have worked on organic farms, operated farm equipment, and have knowledge of crop storage are at an advantage.

Agribusiness

Agribusiness and farm management volunteers work with small farm, co-ops, and non-governmental organizations to teach business planning, marketing, fiscal analysis, and networking.

Successful applicants must have a bachelor's degree in agribusiness or farm management or a degree in business with one year of farming experience. Applicants without a degree must have at least three years of work experience in agribusiness. An extensive knowledge of gardening, business, research, and networking is a plus.

Fast Fact Volunteers receive a living allowance that covers food, housing, and incidentals, enabling them to live in a manner similar to people in their local communities.

Animal husbandry

PCVs who work in animal husbandry (the practice of breeding and caring for farm animals) help farmers provide balanced diets for their families, increase their income, encourage livestock inoculations, establish gardens and beekeeping operations, and instruct farmers in marketing and land use.

Applicants must have a bachelor's degree in animal husbandry, zoology, livestock science, or biology. Applicants can have a bachelor's degree in unrelated fields and a minimum of 18 months of work experience with farm animals.

Applicants that don't have a degree but have a minimum of three years experience working with livestock may qualify. Volunteers with a background in veterinary medicine, a familiarity with gardening, and experience managing businesses may also qualify.

Health

Volunteers in the health field focus on the following:

◊ Health of mothers and children

◊ Diet and cleanliness education

◊ Disease prevention information

◊ Improving sanitation

◊ Increasing the availability of clean drinking water

Twenty-four percent of volunteers work in the health sector.

Successful applicants must have a bachelor's degree in a health-related field or in any field combined with relevant professional or volunteer work. Volunteers who are registered nurses and those who have other health care certificates may qualify.

The following are sub-fields within the Peace Corps' health service area:

Public health

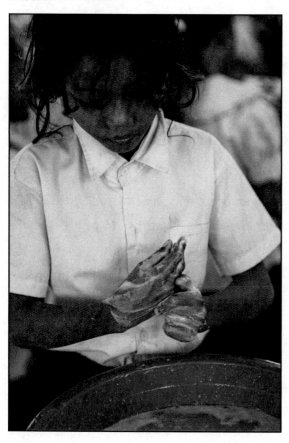

Some volunteers devote their time to community health education. They recruit teachers to inform residents about the health of mothers and children, diet, and sanitation. Volunteers also coordinate activities to raise funds for health supplies, and they instruct peer counselors about STD prevention.

Successful applicants must have a bachelor's degree in any field and a background in public health. Applicants can be a registered nurse, a volunteer or worker in AIDS education, family planning guidance, emergency response, or direct patient care.

Water quality and sanitation

Health volunteers who concentrate on water quality and sanitation help increase the public's awareness of good hygiene practices, build better quality water tanks, and construct latrines.

PCVs can have a bachelor's degree in any field, but must have a minimum of three months of work experience relevant to the field. Volunteers without degrees must have worked in some aspect of construction or plumbing for at least a year. Volunteers should have performed community education related to health or the environment. Applicants should be able to physically endure the requirements of the job.

HIV/AIDS Outreach

All PCVs in Eastern Europe, Africa, Central Asia, and the Caribbean, regardless of the field they specialize in, are trained in HIV/AIDS outreach. Health volunteers might work in orphanages dedicated to children who are HIV-positive, they might develop AIDS prevention programs, or they might counsel those affected by the disease.

Volunteers who specialize in education will teach AIDS care and prevention, instruct peer counselors, and establish support groups for orphans and those who are HIV-positive. Volunteers who work in business development help establish and generate funding for HIV clinics and AIDS education programs.

Information Technology

Interested in green lines of falling numbers, black trench coats, and sunglasses? Go watch *The Matrix*. If you have a passion for technology and helping people, you might be interested in working in the Peace Corps' information technology field. (Don't worry; you can do both.)

Volunteers in this field increase poor communities' access to computers and the internet. They also offer education and technical support to schools, national and local governments, non-governmental organizations, and businesses. PCVs establish databases and computer networks for government offices and businesses, they help business owners and farmers use computers to find new markets, and they help connect schools to the internet.

Successful applicants must have a bachelor's degree in computer science or information systems or a bachelor's degree in communications or any other field — provided they have at least 15 credit hours in computer science and two years of related work experience. Applicants should have at least five years work experience as a computer programmer, systems analyst, or in a related position. Volunteers with an associate's degree in a relevant field or two years in a related discipline may qualify.

Successful applicants must understand fundamental computer functions and have leadership qualities. Experience in web-based sales is a plus. Some applicants will have experience teaching others to make multimedia presentations, writing curricular materials, and developing websites.

Food Security

Food security means making sure that people can get the food that they need. PCVs who work in agriculture, the environment, and health and nutrition are most directly involved in promoting food security. Projects include teaching residents how to garden and farm without destroying the soil, helping communicate between farmers and markets, and helping growers with their business needs.

Peace Corps projects have always indirectly helped communities achieve food security. To help address the worldwide food crisis, the Peace Corps has made food security a special priority since 2008.

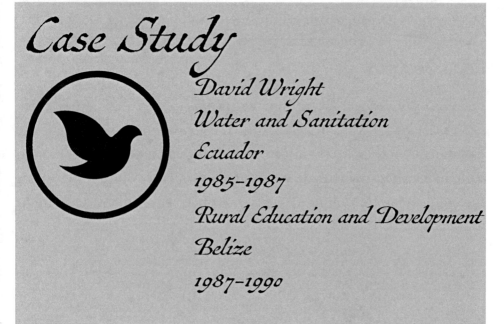

Case Study

David Wright
Water and Sanitation
Ecuador
1985–1987
Rural Education and Development
Belize
1987–1990

One of the images that remains with David Wright after his service in Ecuador is the picture of 17 grown men jumping up and down on a water tank that he built. As a volunteer on water and sanitation projects, Wright helped introduce a kind of water tank construction that used less cement than builders typically used for similar structures. Engineers from Ecuador did not believe Wright's tank would hold up as well. "These Ecuadorian engineers were very skeptical. They said, 'We don't think your tank is very strong, so we're going to get up on top of it and jump up and down,'" Wright recalled.

There are now at least 2,000 similarly-constructed tanks in Ecuador.

Wright left his business as a passive solar heating consultant to join the Peace Corps at age 40. Inspired by a television commercial in which a RPCV described using her cooking and baking skills as a home economics educator, Wright applied to serve as a construction worker. Wright advises prospective volunteers to closely examine their motives for applying to the Corps. He had a successful Peace Corps experience because he realized his pre-service goals of learning a new language, understanding another culture, and becoming familiar with the economic hardships people in the developing world face.

Having grown up in the United States, Wright was unprepared for the slow pace of life and work in Ecuador. The first day Wright walked to work in the small Andean town where he served, he had difficulty adjusting to the slow pace of the townspeople. "I wound up walking in the street and passing everyone," Wright said.

Residents would often ask where he was going in such a hurry. Talking with colleagues required a similar adjustment. In the U.S., work-related conversations often focus on the tasks at hand. In Ecuador, talking business before asking about a colleague's family is considered rude. Employees also generally worked at a slower pace than in the United

States and dealt with problems in a less confrontational manner. "I had to adjust myself to the idea that I wasn't necessarily wasting time or not doing my job," Wright said.

The intercultural openness Wright developed in the Peace Corps has served him well throughout his career. After finishing two terms, Wright took positions supervising and training volunteers. He eventually moved to Southeast Asia to work with the International Rescue Committee and now works in Indonesia as an environmental health adviser with CHF International.

The opportunity to understand how to work and live in another culture makes the Peace Corps especially valuable for people seeking an international career. To get the most out of Peace Corps service, volunteers should remain open to learning from those in their countries of service. "I think it's very important that you do not assume you have all the answers going in," Wright said.

Who Can You Meet?

Fresh-faced college grads with newly-minted degrees are the classic image of PCVs. While it's true that many people still join the Corps right out of college, things have changed since the Peace Corps was founded in 1961.

Today's Peace Corps works to represent the diversity of Americans. Meaning that, if you have something to offer the Peace Corps and meet the basic requirements, nothing — not your age, race, orientation, or education — will stand in the way.

In order to make the Peace Corps a comfortable and safe place for all of its volunteers, it takes a hard stance against discrimination. An EEO (Equal Employment Opportunity) counselor is in place to help those who feel that they have been victimized. The Peace Corps Office of Civil Rights and Diversity will also protect the individual rights of volunteers.

LGBT volunteers

Being something other than straight, even in America, can be tough. Unfortunately, it's even tougher in third world countries — countries that are most in need of the Peace Corps' help. This is why the Peace Corps provides in-country support for LGBT volunteers. This allows LGBT PCVs (the Peace Corps loves acronyms almost as much as it loves civil rights) to connect with a support network of other LGBT volunteers.

"Volunteers should begin gathering information during the segment of pre-service training devoted to cultural attitudes toward race, gender, sexuality, and other identity issues," said Mike Learned, RPCV and site editor, for the Lesbian, Gay, Bisexual and Transgender U.S. Peace Corps Alumni website, **www.lgbrpcv.org**. According to Learned, the Peace Corps medical officer and current PCVs can also be helpful in finding information.

The Lesbian, Gay, Bisexual, and Transgender U.S. Peace Corps Alumni site offers a mentoring program that pairs potential volunteers with RPCVs. The group also provides a ListServ for applicants, which distributes helpful resources to those in need. To subscribe to the ListServ or request a mentor, visit the organization's website at **www.lgbrpcv.org**.

Fast Fact — *Only U.S. citizens can be Peace Corps volunteers or apply for the positions of country director, director of management and operations, director of programming and training, and associate Peace Corps director.*

Volunteers of various races

One of the Peace Corps' reasons for existing is to give residents of host countries a chance to get to know Americans. The Peace Corp is committed to representing Americans in host countries as they are at home.

Stereotypes still exist in other countries, but they differ from the stereotypes with which we struggle. Some host-country nationals do not see minorities as true Americans and occasionally target them for verbal harassment. Host-country nationals in African countries do not acknowledge any ethnic similarity with African-American PCVs. As an American, you will be an outsider and some host-country nationals may treat you with suspicion and contempt. It's important to remember in these situations that 99 percent of the time, your actions will overwrite any biases that natives in your communities hold. So, focus on helping the natives of your assigned country. Your work will speak for itself.

Volunteers with disabilities

Having a disability doesn't mean that you can't join the Peace Corps. In fact, there have been many cases of people with disabilities — including deafness and blindness — being great Peace Corps volunteers.

The Peace Corps will make sure volunteers with disabilities have everything they need to provide effective service, according to the website Mobility International USA (**www.miusa.org**). In the past, they have shipped Braille machines to host countries and constructed ramps in order to make host family's homes wheelchair-accessible. Always speak with a Peace Corps representative before you decide that you aren't fit for service.

Volunteers of many faiths

By now, you probably get the idea that the Peace Core doesn't discriminate against anyone. To clarify, it should also be said the Peace Corps also doesn't discriminate against people based on their religious beliefs.

However, religion can be a very sensitive subject especially in some of the Peace Corps' host countries. To avoid conflict, volunteers must not use their service opportunity to evangelize. This doesn't mean that you can't continue to observe your own religious practices, but if you're delivering sermons from a street corner, you could be dismissed.

Volunteers with work experience

You may not want to hear it, but in most cases, Peace Corps volunteers have college degrees. Eighty-nine percent of volunteers have at least an undergraduate (four year) degree. A degree shows that an applicant is committed and hard-working.

That being said, if you have professional skills, work experience, and a commitment to service, you might not need a degree. Experience in building, farming, tree maintenance, hazardous materials management, and water treatment are especially valuable to the Peace Corps.

Volunteers for water treatment projects need a year of experience in woodworking, construction, plumbing, or stone work. Volunteers in forestry and agriculture need a year of experience at a nursery or fish farm. To be assigned to a project in agribusiness, it is necessary to have spent three years managing a farm or related enterprise. To serve as an environmental or water engineer, applicants must be certified to treat water or sewage, or to handle hazardous materials.

Volunteers with associate's degrees

If you have a strong distaste for higher education and don't have any work experience, you might be able to get into the Peace Corps with just two years of higher education. PCVs with an associate's degree work in positions such as business advising, computer science, and NGO (Non-Governmental Organization) development.

If teaching a trade is something you could see yourself doing, a two-year degree in Trade Education might get you a position teaching technical classes. If you're interested in medical care a LPN (licensed practical nurse) can assist with AIDS prevention and education. There are plenty of opportunities working with in agriculture if you get a degree in agricultural science or animal husbandry. Any two-year degree qualifies a volunteer for an assignment in youth development.

Spouses serving together

Do you have marriage plans on the horizon? Are you thinking about putting off marriage for Peace Corps service? Maybe you're postponing Peace Corps service until a less busy time in your life. If you and your partner both have a passion for service, you could serve in the Peace Corps together after only a year of marriage.

Five percent of volunteers serving in the Peace Corps are married. Because two positions must be found in the same area, couples usually have a longer waiting period than the typical 9-12 months for their assignments. For a married couple to serve together, the applicants must have been married for at least one year before leaving for their assignments. Couples with minor children must document how their children will be cared for and financially supported in their absence.

Fast Fact *Unmarried couples in domestic partnerships can also serve together. They must have been in a committed relationship for a full year before they begin their service and submit an affidavit stating the legitimacy of their partnership.*

Mature volunteers

Maybe you're thinking that this isn't the right time in your life for the Peace Corps. However, there's nothing wrong with serving the Peace Corps late in life. Seven percent of volunteers are over the age of 50. The oldest Peace Corps volunteer, Alice Carter, joined at the age of 86. Volunteers who have spent decades working in their disciplines have a wealth of knowledge to share with their host-country counterparts, and many residents welcome the experience and expertise of the mature volunteer. So, if you decide that the Peace Corps doesn't fit your life now, always remember that it's never too late to join.

Case Study

Donna Statler

Belize

Education

1989–1991

D onna Statler did not have a lifelong desire to join the Peace Corps. In fact, the urge to join took Statler by surprise and was part of a transformation that included getting a divorce and returning to school. Statler's metamorphosis began in her early 30s and continued right until she left for Belize at age 38.

Serving as an ambassador for ordinary Americans was one of Statler's most rewarding aspects of working in Belize. Many host-country nationals picture the U.S. as Hollywood's glamour or Manhattan's excitement, but Statler's agrarian background helped her show the residents of Belize that they might have more in common with people in the U.S. than they imagined.

Statler, who regularly visits Belize, has helped Belizeans study in the United States, and has a scholarship named after her at the high school in her former community of service. Statler is happy to have established international ties with the residents and to have made a good impression on behalf of the United States. "They look at Americans in a positive light," Statler said.

During her time in Belize, Statler witnessed her own self-discovery and personal growth. Forming international ties and connecting with members of her community of service were not the only rewards of serving in the Peace Corps; Statler also underwent a significant amount of personal growth. Learning she could rely on herself and thrive in a foreign country was one of the most meaningful aspects of service. "The most rewarding to me was just that I could make it," Statler said.

Endurance has been a hallmark of Statler's life, and she used her experience as one of 12 children growing up on a farm to demonstrate she could adapt to life in Belize and teach members of an agricultural community. A bachelor's degree with a minor in special education strengthened Statler's application.

Flexibility and the confidence to work without extensive supervision were key qualities that helped Statler succeed as a PCV. As a teacher trainer, Statler taught instructors how to make school subjects more meaningful to students who work on family farms. She also painted classrooms and built desks. Once when a teacher was unexpectedly absent, Statler found herself in front of dozens of 4 and 5-year olds with no books, no electricity, and no lesson plans. Conducting a class in a foreign country without many of the resources that teachers in the States take for granted strengthened Statler's confidence in her ability to adapt and solve problems.

Statler's service in the Peace Corps also made her a stronger candidate in job interviews. The experiences Statler had in the Peace Corps gave her the confidence to apply for jobs that previously she might not have felt qualified to try, including one working with convicted sex offenders. "Before Peace Corps, I wouldn't have said 'I *know* I can do a great job,'" Statler said.

Chapter 4: What the Peace Corps Asks of Volunteers

You know what type of experience the Peace Corps wants in its volunteers. You know what type of service they provide and where. But once you've been accepted into their illustrious folds, what is it exactly that the Peace Corps expects? Part of being a successful volunteer is knowing the job description. Keep the following ideas in mind and you'll be well on your way to completing the goals that attracted you to the Peace Corps in the first place.

Time

Looking forward to the newest installment in *The Fast and the Furious* franchise? If you volunteer for the Peace Corps, you might have to watch it with subtitles or even wait for the DVD release. And let's be honest, Vin Diesel is meant for the big screen.

Perhaps the hardest thing for a potential Peace Corps volunteer to give up is time. The Peace Corps requires each of its volunteers to train for three months before their two-year assignment. For 27 months, volunteers will be separated from their friends and family, possibly without phone or internet exchanges. Two years can be a very long time in a fast-paced world.

It's easy to dedicate yourself to something, but you should also think about the people who rely on you. If you already have children or family that depend on you, you might have to help them before the Peace Corps becomes a possibility. The Peace Corps requires volunteers to document arrangements they have made to financially support their dependents in their absence. Volunteers must also consider if they can make adequate provisions for the care of any sick or elderly relatives for whom they are responsible. In two years a lot of family milestones can go by: graduations, births, quinceañeras, and bat mitzvahs could all pass you by. While the Peace Corps releases members for family emergencies, volunteers should know that family obligations aren't just financial.

In the majority of host countries, stability is in short supply. Something outside of your control could cause your original job assignment to change or become impossible at a moment's notice. This can be daunting to someone who gave up a job opportunity where progress was guaranteed. It's important to remember that, whether or not you end up doing what you set out to do, you will make a difference in people's lives. The time you give to the Peace Corps will always be well spent.

A Desire to Help Others

Being interested in the Peace Corps in the first place shows that you have the desire to help the less fortunate. But a desire to help others isn't like a blood type; it takes work to maintain. A true desire to help those around you means constantly looking for the best way to do your job. Learn from other Peace Corps volunteers and look out for ways to improve yourself. Doing this will not only improve the service you provide to host-country nationals, but it will give you the satisfaction of having done your best.

A Desire to Help the Community

A Peace Corps volunteer is not only a worker. They represent America to the host country that they serve. If you want to reinforce stereotypes about Americans, use your time in the Peace Corps making loud complaints about the lack of fast food or flat screens. Representing the Peace Corps, however, involves befriending those around you.

You should first listen and observe without passing judgment. Many customs and values go against American morals. It's important to remember that the Peace Corps can only lead through positive examples. Putting the community first may mean holding your tongue on subjects such as corporal punishment and the status of women.

To keep community relationships intact, volunteers must also accept accountability for their actions during work and non-work hours. Communities of service are often small and close-knit. Any questionable conduct by a volunteer tends to spread quickly.

Obedience to the Rules

Benjamin Franklin once said, "An ounce of prevention is worth a pound of cure." With medical care being remote in most countries of service, there are few places where this phrase is truer. Peace Corps rules exist to prevent death, injury, or illness to volunteers, and violation of these rules could result in a volunteer being dismissed.

Most volunteer deaths are the results of accidents that could have been prevented by following Peace Corps rules. These rules are common sense, like wearing a helmet on a motorcycle or taking prescribed medication to prevent diseases or sickness. With the exception of alcohol, recreational drugs are prohibited. There are also territories that volunteers are not allowed to enter for their own safety, such as war zones. Peace Corps trainees learn about the laws of their countries of service during training.

A Willingness to Go Anywhere

This sounds like another call to adventure, but most volunteers have a hard time calling outdoor latrines an adventure. In order to see the world, you may have to leave some luxuries behind and accept a leaner lifestyle.

The stipend PCVs receive is meant to pay for food, housing, and modest entertainment. The standard of living it provides is probably a lot lower than you're used to. In many countries of service, walking and cycling are how you'll be getting around. You might stay in a house heated by a wood fire. When you're deciding whether Peace Corps service is right for you, don't only think about seeing the African savannah or hiking the Alps. Also consider whether you'd be willing to live somewhere where a trip to the bathroom means putting on a coat.

Chapter 5: Your Actual Chances of Being Hired

I f the promise of adventure, immersion in a new culture, and enhanced career prospects have piqued your interest, the next thing you'll want to look at is the application process. It can be pretty intimidating looking at it all at once. If you feel underqualified, you can take a few years to gather work experience or take care of that pesky degree. Remember that it's easier to focus on one part at a time when you're actually applying.

So, for now, let's forget the interview, the references, and all the paperwork. To start off, let's just look at...

The Basic Requirements

◊ You have to be at least 18 to apply; there is no maximum age limit.

◊ You have to be a U.S. citizen.

◊ If you have kids, you can't bring them along. Be ready to find a long-term babysitter and a way to provide for them in your 27-month-long absence.

◊ If you want to serve with your wife or husband, wait until after your first anniversary to serve. The Peace Corps requires all couples serving together be married for at least 12 months before their departure date.

◊ Remember that serving with a partner means more work on the recruiter's part and a slimmer chance of getting in. Married couples can strengthen their chances if they are willing to take any assignment. If both partners can speak Spanish or French — languages for which there is a high demand — they are also more likely to find a position.

◊ If you're married and wish to serve without your spouse, you must have documented proof of your partner's consent. The Peace Corps is not a guilt free way to abandon your family.

◊ You have to pass the physical examination.

◊ This involves screening for diseases, which may postpone your service or, if the Peace Corps can't provide the accommodations required under the Americans with Disabilities Act (ADA), disqualify you. A link to the PDF file detailing the medical conditions not covered by the Peace Corps can be found at www.peacecorps.gov/volunteer/health-and-safety/medical-information-applicants.

◊ You must commit to two years of service and three months of training.

Still reading? Good. The actual work starts at this point and doesn't really stop until you're on the plane heading home. Reflect for a moment and, when you're ready, click "Apply Now" to start the application process. (You can actually apply after you've read this. Just imagine clicking the "Apply Now" button if you want; visualization is the first step to realization.)

Fast Fact *Joining the Peace Corps is free! There are no application fees, and the cost of visas, passports, and plane tickets are covered. The only costs some applicants might have to pay are for medical screenings.*

How to Apply

Prospective volunteers can find a link to start the Peace Corps application at **www.peacecorps.gov/apply**. If you're feeling old-school or suffering from computer allergies, contact 1-855-855-1961 or visit a regional recruitment office to receive a paper application. You can also use that number to ask a Peace Corps recruiter any application questions. To find a recruitment office near you, visit **www.peacecorps.gov/volunteer/connect-with-a-recruiter**. To find out more information, attend some of the events listed at **www.peacecorps.gov/events**. You can also connect with the Peace Corps through social media on Twitter, Facebook, Instagram, Pinterest, Tumblr, and YouTube.

The Application Process

On average, the application process can take six to 12 months to complete, but it can take longer because of reference checks, medical evaluations, and the availability of assignments. After being accepted by the Peace Corps, most people depart for their country assignment within two to three months.

Keep pressing next

Before you click (or imagine clicking) the "Apply Now" button, make sure you have your résumé, education history (including GPAs), and your close friend and professional references (their information; not them) at the ready. This is the boring part. You want to save yourself as much torture as possible. Schedule this stage of the application process for a time when you're alert and not as likely to fall asleep on the keyboard.

The online application does not need to be completed in a single session. You will create a profile which you can return to later. The process can be completed in under an hour. However, if you're going for speed records, your time might be better spent playing *Boggle*. The words of the day are *quality* and *thoughtfulness*.

During this stage of the process, you will need to submit the following items:

◊   Your contact info and résumé

◊   This includes your name, citizenship status, and social security number (for a background check). Be sure to tailor your résumé so that experience applicable to the Peace Corps is all up-front and easy to find.

◊   Your background information

◊   This contains a lot of yes or no questions about whether you have any obligations (family, military, or otherwise) or a history of crime. It's probably a good idea to settle up any pending court cases before you start this section of the application.

◊   Education history

◊   This includes your highest level of education, degree, and GPA.

◊   Motivation Statement

◊   This is the essay portion of your application. It's discussed in more detail below.

◊   References

◊   The Peace Corps requires two references: one of a close friend and one professional reference. The professional reference can be a supervisor for a job or volunteer position or it can be a professor.

◊   Racial and ethnic data

- This part has more to do with the Peace Corps' statistics than your actual application.

The essay

Rewind to the "Motivation Statement." Here, you have 500 words to explain why you want to join the Peace Corps and how you would deal with the obstacles volunteers face. Recruiters use this information to get an idea of an applicant's professionalism and maturity. Five hundred words may sound like a lot, but there's a lot of information that you need to convey, so make every word count.

This sample essay answers a prompt asking applicants what inspired them to join the Peace Corps and how this inspiration relates to their history and their goals.

Sample essay

By: Julia Abigale Johansen, Education, Ukraine 2007-2009

Tonight was one of the best nights of my life, and it was exactly the reason I went into teaching ESL. I was invited to dinner by one of my former students. I went expecting a sit down dinner, with maybe four or five people, perhaps six, and instead was treated to an awesome Saudi Arabian dining experience. We had tons of amazing food and engaging conversations. Because we were outside of the classroom, it gave us an opportunity to relate as people in an informal setting. It was a chance for them to show off parts of their culture they are proudest of to one of their teachers. I got to see a slice of Saudi culture that I would not have seen otherwise.I have a true sense of wanderlust. No way would I ever be content staying in the same city, the same state, or even the same country while the world was out there to explore. I know in my heart that just being a tourist would never give me the satisfaction of really being a part of a culture. I am not content with the experience-equivalent of a fast food restaurant; I want to savor my experiences. When I first heard about the Peace Corps years ago, I knew it was exactly what I was looking for. The exchange of culture and ideas is what really breaks down prejudices. Until I started teaching ESL I was not aware of how many prejudices I had, and I am so grateful every day to break down my own stereotypes and the students' as well. I want to know people outside of what the media tells me, not as a tourist, but as an honored guest. People like me, and organizations like the Peace Corps help dispel myths perpetrated by media and tourists. The Peace Corps would give me the chance to experience a people in a way that I would not normally get to and would provide a profound life experience — there is something important that happens during a volunteer experience, doing something out of love rather than out of need for money.I have wanted to teach ESL for about as long as I have wanted to join the Peace Corps, and the reason why I have not tried to do either until now is that I wanted to do them right. They are so important to me that I wanted to make sure I had all the qualifications, all the degrees, all the preparation out of the way. At this point I have finished my master's degree, and am completely qualified to teach anywhere in the world, and I am pausing in embarking on my career for the chance to join the Peace Corps, because I want to start my career by doing something important and significant and not based on how much money I can make. Sure, money is important, but right now for me, the experience is more important, and I would be honored and excited to be accepted into the Peace Corps.

The health history form

Now that you're on a roll with paperwork, you might as well knock this one out too. If you're attentive, you looked over the medical and health information before you began your application and have a head start on this form. If you didn't, take this time to imagine a long, stern glance in your direction.

The health history form is just more information to make sure that you're fit for overseas service. Get used to it. This isn't the last or the most probing of the Peace Corps medical screenings.

The soft skills questionnaire

Here is where you will give the Peace Corps an idea about the type of work and work environment that would best suit you. It's best if this complements the résumé that you provided in the initial application.

The interview

At this point, you're allowed to get a little excited. Your application — just a fish in a school of thousands — was read by a real person and reeled in, gasping, to the shore. You have a great opportunity. Do your research and dress professionally. This one meeting will significantly influence the outcome of your application. Prepare to discuss your inspiration for joining the Peace Corps and your experience. Even if you don't know the language of your preferred country of service, discuss the challenges you overcame while learning any foreign language.

Be prepared for questions outside of a normal job interview. Questions like: What are your methods for handling stress? How would those methods work outside the realm of your usual support system? What are your thoughts on having to change your appearance or habits to adapt to the culture of a host country? Applicants must be prepared to discuss cultural differences and any commitments that would make it difficult to finish their service.

During the interview, recruiters try to have a relaxed conversation that can range from less than an hour to two hours. The hardest thing to do when you're nervous is to appear calm and relaxed. Remember that the recruiter knows how stressful this situation is and expects a little nervousness on your part. It's your job to get past the nervousness and let them know who you are and why you would be a great addition to the Peace Corps.

The invitation

If you are qualified, a placement officer will extend an invitation to join the Peace Corps. You will be provided with a specific country of service and given a job description. You will receive a welcome packet, your date of departure, job assignment, and more. Invitations are typically sent out two to three months — but at least six weeks — before the volunteer will leave for service.

The Peace Corps' travel office will issue you an electronic ticket for travel to your orientation session. You will meet other trainees before leaving for your host country for in-country training.

Medical and legal clearance

The Peace Corps publishes a long list of health problems that usually can't be accommodated in countries of service. These include potentially fatal allergies, metastasized cancer, recurring heart problems, HIV, muscular dystrophy, psychosis, schizophrenia, chronic major depression, and recurrent hepatitis.

Conditions such as cancer and herniated disks could mean waiting before joining the Peace Corps. Even things like pap smears, cystic acne, and waiting for braces to straighten teeth could cause delays.

If you have any of these, you should talk to a Peace Corps recruiter before immediately disqualifying yourself. Your case may be exceptional or the rules may have changed.

If you have debts, you have to prove that creditors will be satisfied in your absence by documenting your plan to pay them. As mentioned before, there are a wide range of options for potential PCVs with student debt. The legal screening also looks into previous lawsuits in which you may have been involved, if you received a dishonorable discharge from the military, divorces, and criminal records. None of these necessarily disqualify applicants, but it helps your chances to be up-front with recruiters. It's always worse for them to hear about your past from a legal screening rather than from you.

Fast Fact

The average age of a Peace Corps volunteer is 28.

Departure

Good job! All the work actually getting in the Peace Corps is done. Now that you have your assignment and your plane ticket you can take a short, but well-deserved rest until you have to go to your in-country training and demonstrate your skills in the field.

Case Study

John Coyne
Education
Ethiopia
1962-1964

Inspired by the idealism of the Kennedy era, John Coyne signed up for the Peace Corps while it was still in its infancy. After two years of teaching English in Addis Ababa, Ethiopia, Coyne spent another two years working as an Associate Peace Corps Director. Coyne's experience as a volunteer and staff member left him with some words of wisdom for prospective volunteers, current PCVs, and those who have returned.

Applicants who are willing to work in any program with a current opening have a better chance at being accepted. Potential volunteers who are willing to serve in any region are also more likely to find themselves holding an invitation packet. Many applicants are college students, but those with five years of work experience in welding, carpentry, and small business ownership also have strong chances of acceptance.

Successful applicants must go beyond convincing the recruiting staff that their skills and interests match open positions. Prospective volunteers should establish credibility by being completely candid.

"The first thing is to be totally honest, because they're going to do a check on you," Coyne said.

Peace Corps staff members evaluate applications individually, but they will rarely accept prospective volunteers with certain life circumstances or medical conditions. Significant medical obstacles include cancer, severe asthma, and major depression. Applicants who have current trouble with the law, who owe large amounts of money, or have children to support, usually will not be accepted.

Succeeding as an applicant requires somewhat different qualities than succeeding as a volunteer. The most successful volunteers are those who have an ironic sense of humor, openness to other cultures, and flexibility. "You cannot be rigid or you'll find out very fast that the American way is not the only way," Coyne said.

After working in what was once a completely foreign culture, PCVs often re-envision their professional lives. Post-Peace Corps work takes different forms for volunteers. Often, people who entered service with a particular passion, find the scope of their interest has become global. So, people who thought they were eventually destined for law school leave the Peace Corps wanting to practice international law. Other volunteers who started service with an interest in business discover they now want to work for an international company.

After returning, Coyne, who has a master's degree in English, edited books on returned volunteers' experiences. Coyne co-founded RPCV Writers and Readers, a newsletter of former volunteers. The newsletter evolved into the website **http://peacecorpsworldwide.org**, which publishes short writings by former volunteers, reviews of books by RPCVs, interviews with authors, and other items of interest to applicants.

Returned volunteers find re-adjusting to life in the United States much more stressful than getting used to life in their countries of service. In their countries of service, volunteers trained with other people who were having a similar experience, but upon returning, some find themselves isolated from friends and family. RPCVs can ease their transition by developing a routine, such as going to work or school, joining an organization of RPCVs, traveling with other volunteers, and writing about their service experience. Some volunteers might find it helpful to continue traveling after their Peace Corps service. Regardless of how they choose to cope with leaving the Peace Corps, volunteers should recognize that it is normal to find readapting stressful. "Readjustment is probably the most difficult part of the whole Peace Corps experience," Coyne said.

Brainstorming For Your Application

All this information can be bewildering, and the result may be an empty brain. "What have you done that will make you useful to the Peace Corps?" doesn't sound like a friendly question. Phrased that way, few people would have an answer ready.

Relax. If you're interested in something, it doesn't always feel like work experience. Afternoons helping your grandpa on his farm, a summer at computer camp, and helping out in your Sunday school are all great experiences that you can talk about on your application.

Still drawing a blank? The questions in these next few sections can prime you for building a résumé that represents you.

What traits does the Peace Corps look for?

The Peace Corps wants a unified picture: someone whose work, life, and volunteer experience make it seem as if they were destined for Peace Corps service. Of course, no one actually lives their life like this. It's your job to paint a picture for them, starting from volunteer experience all the way through to education. Establish a common theme that makes you suitable for service. It's helpful to make this theme specific (you might have always been a teacher or interested in mechanical things and construction) but you don't have to. To give you some ideas, the following is a list of traits that RPCVs and former Peace Corps staff suggest an applicant have:

- ◊ Professionalism
- ◊ Honesty
- ◊ Patience
- ◊ Optimism
- ◊ Self-motivation
- ◊ Emotional stability
- ◊ Physical energy

◊ Openness to sharing other cultures

◊ Leadership and community service experience

◊ Foreign language fluency

Choosing a field for service

Some of the service fields might sound more intriguing than others. To compare your background with the educational and professional requirements of the assignments that interest you, list everything you've done. Start as far back as you can remember and write down the tiniest, dumbest things you can think of. Don't be embarrassed. Most of these won't go on your résumé, but it will help you remember things that will.

After you've got a decent list, write down the skills you needed for each item. When reviewing your experience, think about how you solved obstacles to achieve your goals. Again, start small. It could be that you overcame your habit of sleeping in so that you could work your way to buying a laptop. Maybe you had to overcome shyness to work the cash register at a summer job.

Looking over the service areas, you might find that you're qualified to serve in more than one area. Answer the following questions about each position or hobby to help decide which assignments you should apply to.

◊ What tasks gave me the greatest sense of accomplishment?

◊ What are my most compelling memories of working or volunteering?

◊ If I never had to worry about money, what parts of my job might I do in my free time?

◊ Which parts of this job, volunteer position, or hobby were most challenging?

◊ What did I learn from meeting these challenges?

◊   What character strengths did I develop by meeting these challenges?

◊   What disappointed me about this job, volunteer position, or hobby?

◊   How did the disappointment impact my overall experience?

◊   How did I fall short in this job, volunteer position, or hobby?

◊   Have I remedied these shortcomings?

◊   If I cannot remedy the shortcomings, how would I work around them in the future?

Use the descriptions in Chapter 3 to determine which assignments would most likely offer rewards that were important in previous work, volunteer, or hobby experiences. Choosing an assignment that matches some of your previous experience not only helps to paint a picture for recruiters, but it also helps you to find and pursue the passions that give your life meaning.

Choosing a location

Determining where you would like to serve means taking stock of your preferences and learning about which areas are good matches for your personality, interests, and experiences.

Before reading about the countries in which PCVs work, take some time to reflect on the type of place in which you would fit. Use a notebook for your thoughts so you can review them during your decision-making process.

Peace Corps staff tries to place you in your preferred location, but they can't make any guarantees. You can refuse to go to any location, but once an assignment has been granted, it's unlikely it will be changed. You can, however, increase your chances of acceptance by being willing to go anywhere.

With eight regions, you have options that range from frigid to tropical, rural to urban, and ancient to modern. Some awake to the crowing of roosters, while others rise to morning prayer calls echoing from domed rooftops. You may work in hand-tilled gardens or in cutting-edge computer labs.

Learning from previous travels

Make a list of all the places you have traveled. Be sure to include long journeys or vacations, day trips or weekend camping trips. This list will provide an overview that can help your assessment. After the list is complete, set a timer for five minutes and write down everything you can remember about the experience. You might have to leave some of the questions blank, but try to provide enough information to give yourself a good overview.

◊   What did you expect before you went to this place?

◊   In what ways did the place live up to your expectations?

◊   In what ways did the place differ from your expectations?

◊   What problems did you encounter?

◊   How did you cope with these problems?

◊   What did you find exhilarating?

◊   What did you find tiring?

◊   Were you homesick?

◊   What helped your homesickness?

◊   How often did you see people you knew?

◊   Did you find yourself wanting to stay longer or to leave early?

◊   Could you see yourself living in such a place?

◊   If you had had to stay for several months, would you have preferred a place that was more urban or less urban?

◊   How often did you contact people at home?

◊   If you had to do the trip over, would you want more contact with people at home?

◊   What are some of your most cherished memories of this place?

◊   How similar to your home was this place and how did you react to the differences?

Your responses to these questions will give you some idea of your ideal country of service. Of course, the ideal country does not exist, but having a sense of what your perfect spot would be like can help you choose a location that comes as close as possible.

Fast
Fact
Forty-five percent of volunteers serve in Africa, 22 percent serve in Latin America, 13 percent serve in Asia, 10 percent serve in Eastern Europe/Central Asia, 4 percent serve in the Caribbean, 3 percent serve in North Africa and the Middle East, and 3 percent serve in the Pacific islands.

Rating your requirements

Peace Corps volunteers work in eight regions of the world, so there is a lot of variety in potential countries of service and work assignments. Below is a list of factors to consider when deciding where to serve:

◊   Climate

◊   Degree of development

◊   Access to telephones and internet (it's best to be flexible on this one)

◊   Types of diseases common in this country

◊   System of government

◊   Types of assignments available

◊   Religions practiced

◊   Languages spoken

◊   Terrain

Rate the importance of each consideration on a scale of one to 10 and note any factors that could be deal breakers. For instance, if you have a medical condition that is exacerbated by humidity, you would have to limit yourself to dryer regions.

When Will You Set Off?

"Ready... set... *wait...*" might be a good motto for those applying to serve in the Peace Corps. It can take up to a year to get a response to your application. Filling out the application can take from one hour to a week, depending on the extent of your work history, medical information, and volunteer experience.

Departure dates vary, but your recruiter will provide a general idea of when you can expect to leave. Volunteers often depart several months after they accept their invitation.

Case Study

Lindsay Jenson
Accepted volunteer in an
agricultural extension program in
Latin America

A desire to learn from people who live in developing countries, a longstanding commitment to service, and a taste for adventure were motivating factors for Jenson.

Jenson studied in Mexico and France. She served as an interpreter for workers on her church's school-building project in Nicaragua, so she knew firsthand the value of understanding people of other cultures. Through Peace Corps service, Jenson looked forward to encountering a less consumerist view of life.

Jenson's previous volunteer service and study abroad made her application more competitive, as did her minor in Spanish and her volunteer work within the United States. Jenson had a bachelor's degree in public relations and worked as a volunteer coordinator for Habitat for Humanity through AmeriCorps/VISTA. She recommends that prospective volunteers do as much volunteer work as they can before applying, even if they serve in the United States. Jenson applied in 2007 and then joined AmeriCorps/VISTA to strengthen her chances of acceptance.

Prospective applicants should spend a lot of time gathering information to help them determine whether they are suited to serve in the Peace

Corps and to help them prepare their applications. "Research, research, research. Talk with RPCVs, read the blogs of current volunteers, or go to the library and read books about the Peace Corps and RPCV stories. Applicants can ask their recruiter every question they can think of. The recruiter can also provide contact information of RPCVs in your area," Jenson said.

Reading the accounts of returned volunteers has heightened Jenson's eagerness to begin serving. "I'm excited about the experience and what I'm going to learn about the community and myself," Jenson said.

Chapter 6: Watching Out for Your Health

I apologize in advance to any hypochondriacs. Thinking about entering a new place with different languages and culture is hard enough without considering the strange parasites and diseases that could be lurking in every river or in every bite of rice, lamb, or stew. But there's no need to fear. The Peace Corps is well-versed in the weaknesses of American immune systems. If there are risks of a virus, you'll get the immunization.

On the other hand, vaccines don't make you invincible. Diseases aren't the only dangers that foreign countries hold. You should always be cautious and follow the rules and safety guidelines that the Peace Corps gives you. Caution is more effective than any medicine you can buy, and stupidity is more dangerous than any disease.

Free Health Care

Accidents may happen and immunizations may fail. However, the Peace Corps employs medical officers in each country to provide free care to volunteers. Each medical officer has a fully-staffed physician's office at his or her disposal. In cases where PCVs' work sites are too far away to reach the office, doctors can make house calls.

Peace Corps medical insurance covers all costs associated with medical care. For more minor health issues, volunteers receive a health kit and intensive training in self-treatment. Should volunteers require evacuation to countries with more advanced medical facilities, the Peace Corps will pay for transportation.

The manual *Where There is No Doctor: A Village Health Care Handbook* by David Werner, Carol Thuman, and Jane Maxwell is a useful addition to Peace Corps training. The book is available for purchase at **www. hesperian.info**. Although the primary audience for *Where There is No Doctor* is health workers, advice on topics such as homemade casts, practices that prevent parasitic infections, and how to correctly identify illnesses could help anyone recognize illnesses in early stages or prove useful in the event that an accident occurs.

At the close of pre-service training, volunteers will receive a health kit, with a wide range of first aid tools including pain relievers, syringes, and antiseptics. PCVs in countries in which malaria is prevalent will also receive anti-malarial drugs and medicine.

Medical Statistics

If you're worried about disease or accidents, the Peace Corps publishes an annual report of illnesses and injuries trainees and volunteers experience. It may help to see the actual rates of accidents, rather than letting your fear come up with the numbers.

The Health of the Volunteer Report is published in "Reports" section of the Peace Corps website at **www.peacecorps.gov/about/open-government/reports**.

Eating Safely

Health, safety, and hygiene instruction is tailored to each nation, but some advice applies across many countries of service.

The tap water in many countries is not suitable for drinking because it carries parasites or microbes. Peace Corps volunteers must drink bottled water or use purification kits. Making sure that food is cooked thoroughly is another health warning that will serve volunteers well regardless of their country of service. It has been said that cleanliness is next to godliness. It's corollary that dirtiness is not far from crippling stomach pain and violent intestinal episodes. This should be remembered if you're feeling lax while cleaning up in the kitchen. Always use hot water and soap.

Fast Fact   *No two Peace Corps programs are the same. If a country has been part of the Peace Corps for a long time, its director may run a pretty tight ship. If volunteers only recently started working in a country, they might still be figuring things out. Don't expect your program to be just like your friend's or like that blog you read.*

Protecting Yourself From Crime

Medical concerns aren't the only dangers that can affect volunteer health. Crime is a major concern in poorer countries and many are not fortunate enough to have effective law enforcement. Peace Corps volunteers easily stand out as unfamiliar to natives and may appear wealthy, making them targets for theft and burglary.

The Peace Corps Office of Safety and Security is responsible for helping PCVs stay safe. The office offers comprehensive safety training, determines whether volunteers' living quarters are secure, and designs emergency response methods.

Volunteers must keep in touch with their nearest Peace Corps office and notify staff members when they leave their posts. Each country of service has an emergency action plan, which volunteers learn as part of their training. The plan advises volunteers how to prepare for and respond to emergencies such as wars, earthquakes, and hurricanes. During an emergency, Peace Corps officials will notify volunteers and assist them in getting to safe areas.

As mentioned before, PCVs are forbidden to enter zones the Corps considers too dangerous. Doing so puts their safety at risk. The Peace Corps likes to keep track of volunteers so that, should something happen to them, they can respond as quickly as possible. For this reason, volunteers must notify the Peace Corps before they leave their host country to travel.

Safety and security rules vary by host country. In some countries of service, PCVs may not ride motorcycles without helmets. In others, volunteers can't use taxis at night. In some countries, PCVs must avoid going to the beach alone. All of these rules, as simple as they sound, are essential to the safety of volunteers and could save their lives.

To get a good idea about the frequency and type of accidents that occur in host countries, take a look at the Peace Corps' latest volunteer safety report, found at **www.peacecorps.gov/volunteer/health-and-safety/ safety-and-security**.

It Pays to Know Your Neighbors

Becoming immersed in your host community is crucial to reducing your risk of becoming a victim of a crime and to increasing the response time of medical care. The more your neighbors get to know you and your habits, such as when you typically turn in at night, the more they can look out for you and alert the right people if you're in trouble.

This will also help you get to know a new culture and community and soon call it your own, as well as introducing locals to a friendly, American face. Be mindful of this. Give them a clearer idea of what America is really like.

Chapter 7: Getting Ready to Go

With all the work associated with applying to and interviewing for the Peace Corps, if you actually get in, you may be in shock. Don't let this convince you that you can take a mental break before you get to your host country. OK, maybe a small one. There are many things you need to do before you're prepared to start saving the world. The least among these is packing.

Take It or Leave It?

You may be wondering how it's possible to cram more than two years' worth of gear into 80 pounds worth of luggage. The truth is that you don't need that much. Most of what you need can be bought in your host country.

The Peace Corps will provide a country-specific packing list, but other than that, pack light. I mean it. Where you're going, you don't need roads. All too often, you'll find yourself hiking to your assignment. You should keep this in mind. Anything you wouldn't want to carry on your back for several miles, leave behind. Maybe your bowling or sousaphone skills will be rendered useless, but it won't be worth the chiropractor bills.

Basic toiletries are available in most host countries. Feminine hygiene products sometimes differ, so pack enough for a few months and, if none are available, have some sent as care packages later. Tape, plastic bags, earplugs, and a knife with a can opener attachment are some lighter items that many Peace Corps volunteers don't think about until it's too late.

Don't dump your whole wardrobe into your suitcase. You'll need some professional outfits, quality cold-weather gear (if geographically appropriate), and several pairs of well-made boots and shoes. The rest of your day-to-day wardrobe can be bought once you get to your host country. This will also help you to fit in with the locals.

Some items that may be worth their weight are entertainment options and objects of sentimental value. Host countries might not be as up-to-date with libraries and cinemas. Shortwave radios, CDs, and books are tried and true boredom busters (books can be mailed after you at a discount; don't weigh yourself down with too many). Video games and MP3 players can be brought, but be aware that you may have limited access to electrical outlets to recharge such devices. PCVs should buy a shortwave radio and electricity converters before leaving the United States to ensure quality.

Pictures of loved ones and friends can be conversation-starters with members of your host family, neighbors, and colleagues. They can also help stave off homesickness. But don't bring the whole photo album. As

RPCV Mark Kohn cautions, "The less you bring from home, the easier it will be to make the new country your home," Kohn said.

When leaving for the airport, it's also important to remember your passport and visa. The Peace Corps staff will process your applications for a visa and a PCV passport, for which you do not have to pay a fee. The PCV passport is only valid for three months after your service.

Learning the Language and Culture

Even if you already have experience with the language of your host country, learning enough to speak to members of your host community can be intimidating. But it might not be as hard as you think it is.

Language classes in the Peace Corps are unique and, regardless of how little experience volunteers have with the language of their host country, they will begin to have conversations with a teacher who is a native speaker on day one of their language class. Talking to native speakers gives volunteers the chance to develop practical communication skills they can build on during their two years of service. If you think you need extra help, one-on-one tutoring is always available. The Peace Corps will make sure that you are prepared for your assignment.

Returned volunteers often give Peace Corps language training high marks for helping them hit the ground running in their assignments. After five weeks of training in Nepali, RPCV Darren Miller left with the confidence to travel, get around his village, and teach math, science, and English to high school students.

Practical Guidance and Technical Training

The Peace Corps won't just throw you into a new country with a language phrasebook and expect you to know how to accomplish your assignment and live like a local. Part of the goal of pre-service training is to help volunteers communicate and develop the practical skills they will need to thrive in their new environments as well as more specialized training concerning their area of service.

Practical training helps PCVs understand health, safety and hygiene, and the basics of cooking and keeping house while in their host country.

Volunteers spend about half their training time in technical training, where they practice skills related to their work assignments. Though volunteers typically enter the Peace Corps with education or work experience in their fields, technical training further prepares them for their specific position with lectures, interactive activities, and demonstrations. Here, volunteers learn the fundamentals of their job first and progress to more advanced skills. The technical trainers are usually PCVs who have served in relevant capacities. Tutoring is available for anyone who has difficulty with technical training. After your first year, you will attend an additional weeklong technical training workshop with lectures, demonstrations, and discussions with volunteers who have finished their terms.

Don't think that the Peace Corps expects this technical training to make you an expert. The Peace Corps is still a learning experience. One returned agricultural generalist recalls applying his rudimentary knowledge of animal husbandry in a surprising situation. On the island of Kosrae, one of the federated states in Micronesia, PCV Mark Kohn was asked to help a family new to caring for livestock with their pig, who was giving birth. After consulting an animal husbandry textbook, Kohn decided that the family's pig was ill, so he gave the creature an injection of penicillin. The following day, the healthy sow contentedly suckled her newborn piglets.

"So for about two minutes, I was a hero," said Kohn. He explained that there was no correlation between the penicillin shot and the successful pig's delivery — the sow and nature had done all the work.

Chapter 8: You're In — Now What?

After all the paperwork and screenings, after the interview, and after the intensive language training, you're standing in your assigned country and ready to save the world. But how?

The first thing you'll encounter on your Peace Corps journey, even before airport security, will be anxieties. How can you expect to change lives? How can you become part of a foreign community? How are you going to make breakfast? One step at a time.

The first step to dealing with anxieties is confronting them. In the next section, you'll find an outline of how most PCVs live and work in their host countries. You can see what kind of problems they had and how they solved them. Hopefully, this will ease the tension and leave you more prepared to meet new challenges (and people) and make positive changes in your new home.

If you're still hungry for reading material or still nervous about making a living in your host country, the Peace Corps offers a collection of real stories told by Peace Corps volunteers at: **www.peacecorps.gov/stories**. These first-hand accounts can give you another point of view of the day-to-day life of a Peace Corps volunteer.

Part One: Living

When you say goodbye to your family and friends at the airport, you might also want to offer a heartfelt farewell to your old habits and expectations. Life in a host country will be different from any vacation you've taken and anything you've seen on TV. Part of fitting into a new culture is learning how to redo everything, from greeting people you meet in public to conducting business to eating. Locals are more likely to trust volunteers if volunteers adapt to their way of life. The biggest obstacle blocking your path from being a foreigner and being a member of your host community is relearning how to live.

Housing arrangements

Peace Corps volunteers choose between living alone or living in a house with a host family. Neither choice guarantees reliable electricity or running water. In most places, internet access and landline telephones are a luxury.

Though most PCVs choose to have their own space, you shouldn't dismiss the host-family option. Sharing a house with a host family gives you more opportunities to practice the language and become more immersed in the culture. A native family who agrees to host an American in their home will make it easier to connect with the community. They will also help volunteers deal with the loneliness of living in a new place.

Some volunteers live in temporary housing when they first arrive and move to their permanent homes after taking a few months to get used to their new surroundings.

Fast Fact When new volunteers first get to their host countries, the Peace Corps gives them a "settling-in allowance" so that they can furnish their new homes with household items.

Doing the dirty work

If you don't like doing the laundry at home, you'll hate doing it in your host country, where washers are people and dryers are clotheslines. There is a way around this problem that not only saves you from (most of) the labor, but also benefits the community and opens relationships with the locals.

Volunteers often pay residents of their host communities to help them with chores. This not only develops relationships with your host community, but the extra income can be the difference between a local having food on the table and going hungry.

A short anecdote courtesy of Richard Ireland, who served in Haiti from 1998 to 2001, shows how valuable a little extra money can be for people who live in a poor country. While eating lunch in the home of a mother of 10, Ireland noticed he was being watched. "All of a sudden I realized all the kids were there and they were very quiet," he said. Eventually one of the children spoke up and said that none of them had eaten that day.

Ireland immediately stopped eating and decided to hire the children's mother to cook for him, which helped her provide for her family.

Don't think that this means you escaped all the work. In many cases, locals still expect volunteers to fetch the water, a trip that's probably longer than the one to your laundry room.

Corps cuisine

You probably know how hard it can be to agree on a place to eat. One person isn't excited about hamburgers, but will eat tacos. One person will have anything really, as long as it's strictly vegan and gluten free. Another doesn't really care, but will eat their firstborn before they eat tacos. When you join the Peace Corps, you can wave goodbye to that headache! Trouble choosing a restaurant is one problem you won't have.

Most of the time, meals in your host country will be decided by what's available. If the fishermen were lucky, you'll probably be having fish. If you don't like rice, you'd better like starvation.

How food is prepared depends on the region. Volunteers will find themselves trying new things or becoming very hungry. This isn't a punishment. Food is a way for locals to share their culture and for volunteers to take steps in joining the community.

If you cook for yourself, you can't always count on having a thoroughly modern kitchen. Or even a halfway modern kitchen. Improvisation can be a valuable skill in these situations. Techniques such as using wine bottles as rolling pins and baking muffins in tuna cans may become second nature. A refrigerator might seem like less of a necessity to PCVs who have grown accustomed to keeping their vegetables cool in wet sand. For more tips on culinary improvising, check out the cookbook, *Where There Is No Restaurant* by former volunteers Aimee Clark and Meghan Greeley.

Vegetarianism

Volunteers are welcome to pursue any diet they choose, but in places where food is hard to come by, this can be impractical. Vegetarians and vegans won't have access to the variety of plant-based proteins freely available in the States.

Something else you might think about if you have a special diet are cultural attitudes. Vegetarianism is a foreign idea in many regions. People there wouldn't even consider making a meat-free meal. This can be a problem if locals offer volunteers food. Refusing food is seen as extremely rude in most countries, and deciding not to eat certain things places Peace Corps volunteers in a difficult position.

Pets

Unfortunately for your scaled, feathered, or furry friends, the Peace Corps does not allow animal ride-alongs. But this doesn't mean that you can't have a pet during your service. Many volunteers care for stray animals that populate many host country streets. Volunteers should make sure that their new animal companion is free of disease and parasites before curling up next to them.

Connecting with your host community

When RPCV Donna Statler returns to Belize, where she served as a volunteer from 1989 to 1991, people wave and call out, "Miss Donna!" At the local high school, there is a scholarship in her name. She has helped several Belizeans attend school in the United States.

Statler, who has red hair and fair skin, did not initially feel as though she fit into the village, but during two years of work at the local school, she developed friendships that have lasted her entire life.

Unlike the United States, many host countries focus on community. Residents are happy to welcome volunteers into their circles of friends. RPCV Richard Ireland found out exactly how welcoming people in Haiti were. When word got around that Ireland lived alone, community members visited to ease some of the loneliness they assumed he must feel.

According to RPCV Julie Bradley, who also served in Belize from 1989 to 1991, if you live alone, you can also get to know locals by paying to eat a meal with them. After you develop a relationship, they could invite you to community events such as dances, weddings, and festivals.

Developing relationships with locals not only accomplishes Peace Corps goals and makes completing your assignment easier, it also makes your Peace Corps service more meaningful. It could even change your life.

Connecting with other PCVs

While a volunteer's focus should be on connecting with locals, nothing helps keep homesickness at bay like a chat with a fellow American. Depending on where volunteers are serving, they might see other PCVs daily or only once every few weeks. Volunteers who work in cities tend to have more contact with their counterparts than PCVs in remote areas.

While teaching in Addis Ababa, Richard Lipez, who volunteered from 1962 to 1964, was rarely lonely because he worked in the same city as about 50 other volunteers. However, RPCV Darren Miller, who served in Nepal from 1991 to 1993, had to hike several hours to visit the closest PCV. Making brownies with someone else who understood his craving for them was well worth the trek, Miller said.

If you find yourself in an isolated area and can't deal with the loneliness, you should speak to your supervisor about moving somewhere with more people, advised Lipez.

Case Study

C. Joe Andrews
Falalop, Ulithi of Yap State
Peace Corps Micronesia
2005–2007

One of my greatest accomplishments during my service in the Peace Corps was learning to cut tuba (tooba). At least, that is what we called it on my island. "Tuba," "palm wine," or "toddy," has many different names by those who enjoy it around the world. It is the fermented sap of a coconut tree and was a cultural keystone at my post on the almost mile-wide island of Falalop, Ulithi in the Federated States of Micronesia.

In the evenings on Falalop, I was invited to join the "drinking circle" — a gathering of community leaders discussing current events around the world and planning upcoming events around the atoll. It took me over a year to realize that rather than arrive at the circle as a guest, I could learn how to make tuba and contribute to the evening's drink supply. When I began bringing my own tuba to our drinking circle, word quickly spread that I was no longer a helpful American visitor from California, but rather that I had become a local Ulithian.

My tuba-making skills aside, I was involved in numerous successful community projects and had an incredibly fulfilling assignment teaching science and English at Outer Islands High School, which serves students from neighboring islands as far as 500 miles away. I am very proud of these technical aspects of my service, but they pale in comparison to the perspective gained and the joy I felt through the friendships I made as I became a fixture in a once-completely foreign community.

This is why I value my experience in the Peace Corps over all others. I was given the opportunity to join a new culture, and in doing so, experience a new life.

In the 26 months that I lived on Falalop, Ulithi, I learned what it is to be an Ulithian — not just how to speak the language and the significance of the greeting, "Ho buddoh mongoay" (come and eat!). I got to experience lying on my back singing songs with friends under star-packed skies, joining the men on fishing trips, the destructive nature and blissful fun of small island gossip, and the joy of dancing like a fool at the occasional "fun night" village-wide dance.

Technology

Using a laptop, camera, or phone is a great way to share your Peace Corps experience with friends in the States. It's also a great way to break expensive equipment.

Jolting buses and sweltering savannahs are not technology friendly. Neither are thieves who think that anyone with an American accent has expensive possessions. This doesn't mean you have to leave all your technology at home. It does mean that you should take some precautions.

If devices depend on internet access, you might not be able to use them as often as you'd like. Many Peace Corps countries have internet access, but service can be spotty. You are most likely to be able to get online at an internet café or the Peace Corps office. Volunteers often do not have the option to connect at home or at work.

Consider leaving the digital camera with eight exchangeable lenses at home in favor of something that wouldn't bankrupt you if lost or broken. You might want to use the cellphone that the Peace Corps provides or buy a cellphone in-country. Look for a multi-band cellphone to maximize your chances of getting signal. To ensure that you can use the SIM card of the local service provider in your host country, get a phone that is unlocked.

Fast Fact

Nearly one in three people quit the Peace Corps before their service is supposed to end. Before you apply, be sure that you can you make the two-year commitment.

Keeping in touch with loved ones at home

Believe it or not, once your parents are several thousand miles away, you might start to miss them. Homesickness can be a real problem for volunteers who go months without any contact with fellow Americans. Keeping up with family and friends isn't just important for keeping up relationships, it also keeps volunteers cheerful and motivated.

Mail

If the U.S. Postal Service is snail mail, mail in host countries might be paramecium-swimming-through-several-miles-of-maple-syrup mail. It often takes months for mail to travel to and from countries of service.

Once packages arrive in-country, prying hands in the Customs office often 'lose' goodies from boxes with return addresses in the United States. Try to arrange for hand-delivery by visitors to other nearby Peace Corps volunteers. Aerograms, or air letters, available in most stationery stores, are lightweight and are more likely to arrive unharmed than other forms of mail.

The United States postal service offers airmail M-bags that allow people to send up to 66 pounds of reading materials overseas at a discount. Although volunteers can sometimes use the diplomatic mail pouch at the United States embassy in their country of service, it is best to not count on access to it.

For more information on staying in touch with your family, visit **www. peacecorps.gov/family-and-friends/staying-touch**. The Peace Corps also offers a resource guide for families of PCVs called *On the Homefront.*

Phone and email

Phone and email might be a better bet for getting in contact with the States. Many countries of service have cafes where you can access the internet for an hourly fee, or make international phone calls. Volunteers can use phone cards or pay cash after calling.

Some volunteers purchase phone plans that include international calling. If you have a solid gold island or own the internet, this may be a good option, but for most people, this is too expensive. You may find a more reasonably priced option at hostels, which sometimes offer international phones and internet connection.

In case of an emergency at home, family and friends can reach volunteers toll-free at any time at 1-855-855-1961. This line is used to contact volunteers about family emergencies and inquire about volunteers who cannot be reached through other methods.

Getting around: travel in your region

PCVs are not allowed to take a vacation during the first three months or the last three months of service. During the middle 18 months of their service, however, they are welcome to use their vacation days to travel anywhere that is not restricted (as mentioned before, the Peace Corps restricts travel to certain regions for the safety of its members). For every month of service, volunteers earn two vacation days.

Volunteers' passports indicate they are in the Peace Corps. Volunteers are not eligible for diplomatic passports.

Case Study

Richard Ireland

Haiti

1998–2001

A deeper understanding of a different culture and lasting ties to his community of service are some of the most treasured aspects of Richard Ireland's years as a PCV in Haiti. Haitians live more communally than many people in the United States, and they were eager to help Ireland become part of their society. "In Haiti, people live outdoors. So you sit on the front porch and you're a part of everybody's life," Ireland said.

Through close relationships with neighbors, and his knowledge of French Creole, Ireland grew to understand Haitian attitudes toward everything from personal space to their ability to control their own lives. Haitians tend to assume that other people want attention and company, so their interactions sometimes surprise Americans who usually place a higher value on privacy and solitude. "I'd be sitting in my room and I'd look up and there'd be somebody standing there staring at me who I'd never seen before," Ireland said.

Ireland's job was to help residents find a job or start a business, but the 75 percent unemployment rate made it impossible for him to keep up with the constant requests for assistance. Having worked as a community service group organizer, a massage therapist, and a body-centered psychotherapist, Ireland knew the emotional rewards of helping others solve their problems. Recognizing that he couldn't help everyone was one of the most stressful aspects of service. Residents' poverty showed on a daily basis. Ireland knew a woman who did not know from day to day whether she would be able to feed her family dinner. "It would be in the evening and there was nothing she could do, so she'd start singing," Ireland said.

Part Two: Working

The Peace Corps can be fun. It means mixing with locals at festivals. It means making friends. But it also means a lot of work. Volunteers are sent out to help the locals of their host countries. A lot of the time, this means, you know, helping. So put down the camera. Set your alarm to sometime before noon. Even if there's not always someone there to tell you so, you've got a job to do.

Punching the Peace Corps time clock

As a volunteer, most of your time will be spent working and building relationships with your host community. Some projects have more vague goals and can vary in their requirements. Other projects, such as running an AIDS testing clinic or teaching elementary school require more regular hours. In some places, hours depend on when the locals are free from agricultural duties. Whatever project you get, passion is the important thing. The hours don't matter as much as doing your best to accomplish something meaningful.

Becoming your own boss

The Peace Corps does not babysit its volunteers. This means that you are the one responsible for completing work. The higher-ups in the Peace Corps will know if you've been slacking off on your project, and you will hear from them if they find that you haven't been doing your job. Again, caring is the important thing here. If you don't care about what you're doing or the people around you, it's easy to be lazy and waste resources that people desperately need.

Fast Fact: In 2015, the Peace Corps received more than 23,000 applications.

Peace Corps paychecks

Once you get your hands on some money, don't go Scrooge McDuck-eyed and wake up three days later with a karaoke machine and an all-leather wardrobe. Funds are limited. Volunteers are given enough money for lodging, meals, transportation, and modest forms of entertainment. The money you get from the Peace Corps is calculated to give you the same standard of living as your neighbors. Make sure you have food before you go on a spending spree.

If you do end up overspending, you can still get money from home. Wire transfers are available in most countries of service. If you have internet access, PayPal charges lower fees than most wire services.

The stipend we talked about earlier is paid out to a bank if a reliable one is nearby. If not, you'll receive your paycheck by mail or by courier. You can also accept your money at the nearest Peace Corps office.

Finding a bank can be tough in an unstable area. Talk to the people in the community. If they use their mattress as a savings account, it might be a sign that the local bank is a hard pass.

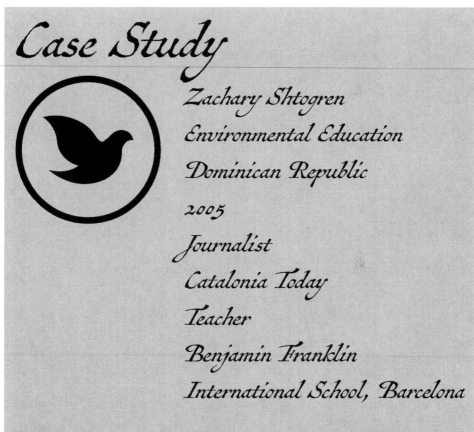

Case Study

Zachary Shtogren

Environmental Education

Dominican Republic

2005

Journalist

Catalonia Today

Teacher

Benjamin Franklin

International School, Barcelona

Learning from a wrong turn could best summarize the value of Zachary Shtogren's time in the Peace Corps.

Inspired by a professional interest in international development, as well as generosity and desire for adventure, Shtogren served as an environmental educator in the Dominican Republic in 2005. Even though Shtogren found the language and cultural training classes rigorous, the technical training did not go beyond what he had learned in introductory college courses.

The emphasis on interpersonal aspects of Peace Corps work continued past pre-service training. Volunteers typically focus on establishing intercultural ties rather than accomplishing concrete development goals. Those looking to begin a career in international development should consider other avenues.

The impact volunteers have on their host communities varies widely, regardless of professional qualifications. Shtogren, who has a degree in environmental studies and worked as an environmental educator before joining the Peace Corps, grew disenchanted with the Peace Corps and began to question the program's overall efficacy.

"The agency has approximately a 30 percent annual drop-out or 'early termination' rate. Any real-world overseas development organization losing this many of its staff a year would be taking a very hard look at its effectiveness," said Shtogren, who now works as a journalist and teacher.

Although Shtogren did not find the Peace Corps useful for the purpose of finding work in international development, he noted that it can strengthen the résumés of those looking for government jobs or any positions in the public sector.

Potential applicants should assess their characters before beginning the application process. "The most successful volunteers are those who are patient, emotionally resourceful self-starters," Shtogren said. So many different positions are available that applicants with varied backgrounds have a strong chance of acceptance. Prospective volunteers can strengthen their applications by presenting themselves as optimistic and energetic.

Those applying should fully understand the nature of the organization. Shtogren said that the most rewarding part of his service was "realizing the Peace Corps is fundamentally a goodwill tour for young people and a hiring platform for the Department of State." If you're someone who can't accept that your goals may be subject to change, then the Peace Corps might not be for you.

Chapter 9: Coming Back Home

You'd think that after two years without modern appliances, the average American volunteer would be sprinting to the tarmac, suitcase flying behind them. Actually, most volunteers find it difficult to leave their host country. Volunteers have to part with two years' worth of friends and neighbors that are more like family. For two years, they've adjusted to an entirely different way of living. Reentering American life can be as difficult as it was to leave it.

Richard Ireland, who served in Haiti, compared the experience of returning to the United States to merging into 80 mph traffic going 25. Life in less developed countries moves at a different pace. After getting used to this, it can be hard to go back to the old way of living. A lot of Peace Corps volunteers can feel out of place in their own homes. It's understandable; for years they've lived lives that most Americans can only imagine. "When you come back, you've had this incredible experience and it's hard to tell people about it," Ireland said.

But Peace Corps volunteers are adaptable. If you adjusted to life in a country whose language you couldn't speak before you started training, you can definitely adjust to coming back home.

Common Stresses of Re-Adjustment

Returned Peace Corps volunteers can find all kinds of problems waiting on them when they come back home. For two years, they've only talked to family and friends from thousands of miles away. That distance can come between people, even people who have known each other for their entire lives. RPCVs can feel lonely and isolated when they first return to the States.

It may be hard for your average American to believe, but after being robbed of shiny, American appliances and bright grocery store aisles, RPCVs can find all the noise and options overwhelming. After leading a simple life, so much excess looks unnecessary. "Grocery stores and toy stores just seemed really obnoxious," said Julie Bradley (PCV from 1989 to 1991).

RPCVs who felt lonely and isolated after their assignments have a few techniques for dealing with these problems. Storytelling is a natural way to get closer with family and friends. When you come back, everyone will want to know what you've been up to for two years, but be careful to space it out. "Most people just wanted the 30-second version," said Bradley. "And that was difficult."

Reaching out to fellow RPCVs can also be helpful in dealing with feelings of isolation and shock. There are RPCV organizations that you can join where fellow volunteers are happy to share the intense experience of two years of Peace Corps service and the troubles that they have readjusting to American life.

All this will help, but it takes time to get back into the swing of things. Bradley suggests giving yourself three or four months to transition back into American culture. The Peace Corps won't leave you hanging here. Volunteers receive a readjustment stipend of $225 per month of service after they finish their term in the Peace Corps. If you finished your full two years of service (and you really should) you'll be getting just over $6,000, which you can use for whatever you like. So, for a while, don't stress about money. Take some time to reflect on the great experience you've had.

Case Study

Kristin Webster

Romania

The first few months of my service were delightful. I was still excited about being accepted into the Peace Corps and everything seemed interesting because it was still new. With Peace Corps staff and other volunteers around, I did not feel the isolation that often happens on site. I was glad to have such an affectionate host family.

It is hard to quantify the things I learned. I learned things like traditional cooking and dancing and even took up knitting with some of the local senior citizens. But I also learned how to be a quicker problem solver, to live independently, to budget effectively, and to be a better and more creative cook, among other things. Of course, 27 months of immersion in Romania also provided me with a solid education in legends, history, folk beliefs, and a great appreciation for a culture I had previously known nearly nothing about.

I only returned about three months ago, and I am still struggling with adjusting. I often feel like it is hard for me to relate to people I meet because so few people seem to know what the Peace Corps is, and they know even less about Romania. It gets frustrating that for the past two years of my life, Romania was the center of my world, and yet it is so far in the periphery for the average American. And as far as Peace Corps countries go, Romania does not seem remotely exotic. I understand why the third goal of Peace Corps is to share the countries we serve in with people back home.

Keeping in Touch with Other RPCVs

Forgot to Facebook your Peace Corps buddies? Didn't have signal to follow them on Twitter? No worries. The National Peace Corps Association website, **www.peacecorpsconnect.org**, has plenty of opportunities to connect with fellow RPCVs. Local RPCV organizations hold potluck dinners, film screenings, and workshops on international business opportunities.

If you find yourself at a loss without some type of service in your life, the National Peace Corps Association also offers plenty of service opportunities. Continuing service will also give you the chance to get to know former volunteers. Returned volunteers mentor teenagers, discuss their Peace Corps experience in public school classrooms, coordinate museum exhibits, and host parties for departing PCVs.

The Peace Corps website offers information to help RPCVs stay in touch. On their site, you can update your personal information in the Peace Corps records, receive past and current issues of RPCV Update, the newsletter just for RPCVs, submit a story about your time with the Peace Corps, learn about joining the National Peace Corps Association, and find how to get copies of your Peace Corps records. You can find all this information and more by visiting **www.peacecorps.gov/returned-volunteers/stay-connected**.

Fast Fact *The Peace Corps can help you learn seldom taught and in-demand languages such as Mandarin, Arabic, Russian, Swahili, and Urdu. Knowledge of these languages can help prepare volunteers for a career in linguistic research, teaching, translation, or intelligence. PCVs also learn more common languages like French and Spanish.*

Keeping in Touch With Locals

Although you'll say goodbye to the natives of your host country when you finish your service, that doesn't mean that you have to say goodbye forever. Many RPCVs develop lifelong friendships with host-country nationals that they maintain by email, telephone, and periodic visits. Former volunteers often find that their communities welcome them back with open arms, despite spending years apart.

RPCVs sometimes host visitors from their host countries and even sponsor the visas for those who want to study in the United States. Keeping in touch with host-country residents helps returned volunteers transition back to life in the States by providing a way to remember their service. In the rush of life in the States, too often the experience of the Peace Corps can seem like a dream.

Case Study

Darren Miller

Education

Nepal

1991–1993

A childhood spent in Egypt set the stage for a lifelong appreciation of international adventure for Darren Miller.

When his college career services office advertised an internship with the Peace Corps in Nepal, Miller could not wait to apply. As Miller waited for word on his acceptance, he became more fascinated by the natural beauty of the country and enchanted by the warmth of its inhabitants. When he learned that the Peace Corps had accepted his application and had assigned him to serve as a secondary school teacher in a village, a seven day walk from the nearest paved road, Miller was overjoyed.

In spite of his affinity for the country and its people, Miller recalls feeling out of place when he first arrived. Seventeen years later, Miller recalls the moment the Peace Corps Jeep dropped him off. "It was a mix of loneliness and then excitement about this big adventure," Miller said.

He grew less lonely soon after he greeted his host family. They welcomed him into their home, and the villagers welcomed him into their social lives. Dancing, drumming, and incense were hallmarks of the eight weddings Miller attended during his first month in the village. Nepalese noticed the differences of religion and wealth between them and Miller, but reacted with tolerance and humor. Miller sometimes attended a Christian church established by missionaries, and members of his Hindu host family asked friendly questions about his faith.

When a friend from the village saw Miller's seven pairs of underwear drying on the balcony, he teased Miller about his wardrobe. "So one of those is for you. What are the other six for?" the friend asked.

Not only did Nepal's economy differ from the United States by being less consumption-oriented, it also differed by being more focused on farmers. On Miller's first day at school, he found only the headmaster present. Other students and faculty were still at home, working on farm chores.

A relaxed attitude towards schedules and time were common in Nepali culture. Nepalese would respond to problems with a calmness that would leave an American fuming. The driver of a bus on which

Miller was riding stopped the coach, got off and left for an hour and a half; when he returned he was carrying a bag of laundry. Although the driver had not announced the reason for the stop, the passengers waited patiently in his absence.

Succeeding as a Peace Corps volunteer often depends on a willingness to adapt cheerfully to the unfamiliar. Prospective volunteers should emphasize their ability to keep an open mind regarding people who grew up outside the Unites States, and they should cite any cross-cultural volunteer work they have done.

To succeed in post-Peace Corps life, Miller suggests keeping in touch with other returned volunteers to share stories and struggles. RPCVs should continue internationally oriented volunteer work, such as donating time to a refugee assistance project to help with the transition. Soon after returning, Miller and a friend from the Peace Corps took a bike tour during which they spoke to students about their service. The warm welcome Miller received reminded him of the kindness he experienced in Nepal and it also made him glad to be home. "It renewed my faith in America," Miller said.

Chapter 10: Peace Corps Alternatives

So you didn't make it. You've had yourself a good cry. You've cursed the Peace Corps, their impossibly high standards, and their impersonal selection process. But just because you didn't make it this time, doesn't mean you can't apply again when you have a little more experience. Even if you decide that the Peace Corps isn't for you, there are plenty of other programs you can join and ways you can help.

The following sections are not only useful for finding an alternative to the Peace Corps, they're also useful for people who think their résumé needs a little more padding before they dive into the Peace Corps application. So wipe those tears away. There's plenty of service to go around.

Fast Fact Fellow RPCVs can be job resources! If they work in the same field, they can keep you informed about of who is hiring and advise you on how to set yourself apart from other candidates. Returned volunteers who collaborated with you while you served can also be used as professional references.

Why the Peace Corps Might Pass You By

Let's not treat this section as dwelling on the past. Dwelling on past wrongs can turn you into an angry, bitter person — possibly a supervillain. Instead of finding an arch-nemesis, treat this as a way to foolproof your application against future rejection.

Keep in mind that getting rejected might not be you or your fault. You may have a great set of skills, but the Peace Corps didn't have the projects to match those skills. It's also possible that the Peace Corps didn't have any assignments in the countries that you picked. You're more likely to be accepted if you aren't too picky about your location or assignment.

If you were rejected because of large amounts of debt or children with no means of support, you were likely told this was the reason you couldn't make it. In this case, the solution to the problem might involve waiting until you have a little more financial stability.

If your application made the cut, but you didn't pass the interview phase, you might want to practice your interview skills. You can always hold mock interviews with friends. Sometimes, the only difference between a successful interview and getting a rejection letter is being confident in your own abilities.

Finding an Alternative Program

Finding a service program is about as easy as finding a stray cat. But before you adopt a cat, you want to check out its motives, how it gets its money, and its reputation with the people it works with. OK, so the metaphor breaks down almost immediately. Just keep in mind that a service program needs to be thoroughly vetted before you decide that it's worth your time. You don't want to go looking for a housecat and find yourself with a raccoon who will take your money without helping anyone.

Spend some time on the internet and find out what kind of reputation a service program has. Most well-known programs are non-profit. If a program makes money, then you should take a closer look. What kind of relationship does the program have with the people it claims to help? Another good thing to look for is if a program covers any costs of your volunteering. Sometimes they'll pay for your plane ticket or cover your living expenses.

After you find out if the alternative program covers any costs, it's time to budget. Think about the cost of airfare, in-country travel expenses, food, housing, and vaccinations. College fellowships and private grants are some other possible sources for funding your trip.

Short Stints

If two years is too much for your fast-paced life, a program that allows you to serve abroad for one to several weeks might be a better fit. These types of programs are perfect for summer breaks, perhaps between graduation and starting your career.

Many programs accept volunteers on a rotating basis throughout the year. Assignments could include restoration of culturally significant buildings, digging at archaeological sites, educating residents about AIDS prevention, working on organic farms, constructing houses, or teaching English. In addition, host-country residents are often happy to help volunteers learn about their culture and language. Volunteers can return home with the satisfaction of knowing they worked on a project intended to better the lives of their new friends.

Spring Break Programs

Tired of the usual spring break scene? Hanging out on the beach is nice in theory, but it's hot, ocean water is salty, and sand is coarse and gets everywhere. Skin rubbed raw by sand doesn't feel great in the ocean either.

Spring break service programs, on the other hand, offer sightseeing, language lessons, and a crash course in another country's culture. Volunteers on alternative spring breaks can serve in a lot of different functions. Some projects include building playgrounds, saving turtles, constructing houses, or conserving rainforests.

The United Way offers alternative spring break programs through which participants can volunteer to help victims of natural disasters continue to rebuild their lives or assist with community development in cities and towns across the country. For information, see **www.unitedway.org/get-involved/groups/student/alternative-spring-break**.

Break Away coordinates alternative spring breaks during which volunteers can work with projects focusing on homelessness and education. For information, see **www.alternativebreaks.org**.

Cross Cultural Solutions runs one-week spring break programs in other countries. These programs combine volunteer work with cultural experiences and language lessons. For more information, visit **www.crossculturalsolutions.org**.

Exchange Programs

If you're less focused on volunteer work and more interested in learning about other countries and seeing the world, college exchange programs might be for you. Most colleges have an international office where you can look into study abroad options. Be sure to ask about the language requirements, required courses, if your credits will transfer, and if the price of tuition is different. Costs differ among programs. In some cases, students don't pay any more for tuition and living expenses than they would in the United States.

Graduating high school can be exhausting for some, especially with the prospect of higher education looming ahead of you. There's nothing wrong with taking a short break. You could also apply for a gap year program. A gap year program will allow you to take a break before going to college, or even between years of college, while you volunteer or study abroad. A lot of students find that this allows them time to figure out what they want to do in life and leaves them better prepared for college.

The Rotary Club offers a Youth Exchange Program for students aged 15 to 19. This program is focused on giving other countries a better understanding of our culture and giving its participants a better understanding of their host country's culture. They also allow families to host foreign exchange students. If you're interested in participating in the Rotary Youth Exchange, log on to **www.rotary.org** for more information.

Transitions Abroad is an information resource for people who want to study, volunteer, or work abroad. The transitions abroad website at **www. transitionsabroad.com** lists study-abroad programs ranging from journalism classes in Prague to martial arts training in Thailand to language immersion programs in France to archaeological digs in Jordan. In addition to opportunities, this site also gives potential travelers resources for settling or volunteering in another country.

Fast Fact

Peace Corps volunteers will have access to the American Club of their country's U.S. embassy. The American Club is a recreational facility featuring familiar food, sports facilities, television, and movies.

People to People Ambassador Programs

People to People Ambassador Programs (**www.ptpi.org**) offers short-term travel programs for students, athletes, educators, and professionals. Ambassadors travel abroad for two to three weeks in groups of approximately 35 as a way to foster local and global networking. They participate in cultural exchange and humanitarian activities and tour culturally significant sites. For professionals, the organizations offer the opportunity to spend about a week in another country visiting workplaces and talking with others in their field. Trips also include sightseeing and home visits.

Case Study

Julie Bradley

Education

Belize

1989–1991

Potential applicants should pay attention to even the smallest inklings that they might want to join the Peace Corps and recognize the variety of locations for service. Posts vary according to degree of remoteness and level of development so applicants can ask to be placed in a country where they would feel at home for two years.

Prospective applicants should not be intimidated by the length of time the Peace Corps asks them to serve. "Two years is not long at all in the grand scheme of things," said Bradley, who joined the Peace Corps after watching a recruiting film at the University of Northern Iowa, where she was studying elementary education.

Offering Belizeans a chance to get to know an American and developing friendships in the town in which she served were some of the most important results of Bradley's service, she said. The children in the agricultural community where Bradley served could identify with her childhood on a farm. Family is so central to Belizean society that residents of Bradley's host community were shocked that she would voluntarily spend two years away from her relatives. "I really liked the fact that I got the chance to dispel some of the myths about the United States," Bradley said.

In addition to myths about the United States, Bradley tried to dispel myths about women's abilities. Bradley went to Belize as a teacher trainer, but the principal initially refused to allow her to hold instructional sessions for the faculty.

"In my school, the principal was pretty chauvinistic and I was pretty young, and he couldn't imagine that I would know anything more than he did," Bradley said. Her initial reaction was anger, but Bradley realized that had he not requested a Peace Corps volunteer, she would not have had a position at his school.

Bradley began by teaching English as a second language and eventually held a teacher training conference on reading instruction. Bradley continued her career in education after leaving the Peace Corps by teaching in Colorado and later in Bolivia. Employers were impressed with the strength of her Peace Corps service. "I think it automatically makes people say, 'Wow, she must be really dedicated and really adventurous,'" Bradley said.

Conclusion

So you're sitting at home in your room or on the bus reading this conclusion. In the back of your head, you're thinking, "Is that it?" It's easy to think of the Peace Corps as a lot of paperwork and rules. You might make the mistake of only thinking of it as a career opportunity. It's true that you won't find a better opportunity to learn skills, but this isn't what the Peace Corps is about.

The Peace Corps is about learning the differences between cultures, their languages, and customs. It's about teaching people in other countries how American culture differs. But more important than our differences are our similarities. The Peace Corps shows its volunteers and the people it serves that we have the same needs and desires.

But if Peace Corps volunteers taught and learned everything they could about different cultures and never helped anyone, the Peace Corps would be failing at completing its most important goal: helping people in need.

While you're bored at home wondering what to do, or you're in class daydreaming about being anywhere else, there's an empty schoolhouse in the Alps and children who would fill it if they had a teacher.

There's a village in Africa where the villagers suffer from stomach cramps and deadly diseases because they don't have access to clean drinking water.

You're on the threshold of a community of heroes that stand up for the sick and young and suffering, no matter how far away. So you want to join the Peace Corps? What are you waiting for?

 # Glossary

Administrative Separation	When the Peace Corps director ends the service of a PCV.
Associate Peace Corps Director (APCD)	The Peace Corps staff member who reports to the country director. The APCD is responsible for helping with the supervision of staff and volunteers. The APCD also assists with the design and assessment of programs.
Completion of Service	When a volunteer finishes their two years of work that they signed up for.
Country Director	The Peace Corps staff member who oversees the program, staff, volunteers, and budget of a country of service.
Country of Service	A country where Peace Corps volunteers work.
Health Status Review Form	The form where applicants describe any health problems.
Home-of-Record	A Peace Corps Volunteer's permanent residence.

Host-Country National	The people who live a country of service.
In-Service Training	Training that volunteers get after they have been in the Peace Corps for one year.
Invitation	The information package that successful applicants receive after their medical papers are cleared and they have a successful interview.
Medical Evacuation	When volunteers are transported to another country to be treated for a medical condition that their host country can't treat.
Medical Kit	Container of first-aid supplies, syringes, medicines, etc. that Peace Corps volunteers receive before reaching their posts.
Medical Separation	When Peace Corps volunteers have to end their service because of injury or illness.
Nomination	The recruiter's suggestion of what program and region that a volunteer should serve in.
Non-Competitive Eligibility	This describes how returned Peace Corps volunteers get advantages when applying to federal jobs.
Peace Corps Medical Officer	A medical professional who cares for the health of Peace Corps volunteers.

Peace Corps Volunteer Leader	A Peace Corps supervisor who helps volunteers adjust to their country of service and interact with their co-workers.
Pre-Departure Orientation	Three-day training in the United States that PCVs undergo before leaving for their countries of service.
Pre-Service Training	Three months of in-country education in the language and culture of the host country combined with training in the jobs volunteers will perform.
Settling-In	Refers to the time after PCVs arrive in their host country when new volunteers set up their living quarters and ease into their jobs.
Staging	Refers to the orientation session that PCVs attend before leaving for their host country.

Additional Resources

www.peacecorps.gov

The official website of the Peace Corps. Features volunteers' memories of service, including a database that is searchable by country of service, program, and other terms. The site also offers an online application with detailed instructions for each step.

www.rpcv.org

The website of the National Peace Corps Association, a networking organization for returned volunteers. The site offers job listings, links to local chapters, and *WorldView*, an online magazine of news and writings from countries of service.

www.peacecorpsworldwide.org

This site features short writings by returned volunteers, lists of public readings, Peace Corps books, and author interviews. Co-founded by returned volunteers, the site lists and reviews books by RPCVs.

www.lgbrpcv.org

The website of the Lesbian, Gay, Bisexual and Transgender U.S. Peace Corps Alumni publishes articles on such issues as support in host countries and opportunities for activism. Prospective volunteers can also request mentors through the site.

www.peacecorpsonline.org

This site provides news about the Peace Corps and returned volunteers. The Peace Corps Library pages include news items organized by country of service, directories of returned volunteers, and historic documents such as annual reports.

So You Want to Join the Peace Corps by Dillon Banerjee

Written by a returned volunteer who served in Cameroon, this book offers brief but informative answers to common questions about applying and serving. Appendices provide information on application requirements for each program, tips on improving the chances of acceptance, and a list of alternative programs.

Bibliography

"Airmail M-Bags: Airmail M-Bags Deliver a Large Amount of Mail to a Single Addressee." **www.usps.com/international/mbags.htm**.

Backhurst, Paul. *Alternatives to the Peace Corps: A Guide to Global Volunteer Opportunities Eleventh Edition*. Food First Books. Oakland, California (2005).

Banerjee, Dillon. *So, You Want to Join the Peace Corps: What to Know Before You Go*. Ten Speed Press. Toronto, Ontario (2000).

Banerjee, Dillon. *The Insider's Guide to the Peace Corps: What to Know Before You Go Second Edition*. Ten Speed Press. Berkeley, California (2009).

Bradley, Julie. Personal interview. May, 2008.

"Burkina Faso: Destination Information." **www.lonelyplanet.com**.

"CIA World Factbook." **www.cia.gov/library/publications/the-world-factbook/index.html**.

A. Clark and M. Greeley *Where There Is No Restaurant*. Friends of Guinea (2004).

"Coming Out: Part One," *British Broadcasting Company*. July, 2007.

"Coming Out: Part Two," *British Broadcasting Company*. August, 2007.

Coyne, John. Personal interview. May, 2008.

2006 Essential Guide to the Peace Corps (CD-ROM), Progressive Management, 2006.

"Frequently Asked Questions." **http://ieo.okstate.edu/ieo. aspx?page=79**.

Green, J. L., "The Nitty Gritty." April 3, 2007 **http://joyagreen. blogspot.com**.

Hachmyer, Caitlin. *Alternatives to the Peace Corps: A Guide to Global Volunteer Opportunities Twelfth Edition*. Food First Books. Oakland, California (2008).

Hastings, T. *The Peace Corps*. Chelsea House Publishers, Langhorne, Pa. (2005).

"International Travel" **http://travel.state.gov/travel/travel_1744. htmlwww.state.gov**.

Ireland, Richard. Personal interview. April, 2008.

Jenson, Lindsay. Personal interview. May, 2008.

Kohn, Mark. Personal interview. May, 2008.

M. Learned, "Peace Corps Equal Opportunity Policy." **www.lgbrpcv. org/articles/eeo.htm**.

Lipez, Richard. Personal interview. May, 2008.

Mc Carron, K.M. "Job Corps, AmeriCorps and Peace Corps: An Overview." July 16, 2002, **www.bls.gov/opub/ooq/2000/fall/art03. pdf**.

Miller, Darren. Personal interview. May, 2008.

"The Monarchy." **www.lesotho.gov**.

"NPCA Calendar of Events." June 9, 2008, **www.rpcv.org/pages/ calendar.cfm**.

"Peace Corps Manual." April 28, 2008, **www.peacecorpsjournals.com/ manual**.

Presley, Sarah, "Teaching English (and More) in Morocco." **www.miusa. org/publications/freeresources/musl imworld/englishinmorocco? searchterm=Sarah+Presley**.

Scheib M., "Volunteering in the Peace Corps (Paraguay)." **www.miusa. org/ncde/stories/buckscamacho?searchterm=Camacho**.

Shtogren, Zachary "Peace Corps Book," Email message. May 19, 2008.

"So You Wanna Join the Peace Corps." **www.soyouwanna.com/site/ syws/peacecorps/peacecorps.html**.

Statler, Donna. Personal interview. May, 2008.

"Travelers Health: Destinations." **wwwn.cdc.gov/travel**.

B. Williams, *The Kingfisher Reference Atlas.* Larousse Kingfisher Chambers, New York, N.Y. (1993).

D. Werner, C. Thuman, and J. Maxwell *Where There Is No Doctor.* Hesperian Books, Berkley, Ca. (1992).

Wright, David. Personal interview. June, 2008.

All images courtesy of the Peace Corps
http://medialibrary.peacecorps.gov/032516ogilvy

Index

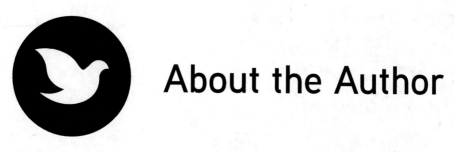

About the Author

Luke Fegenbush is a University of Kentucky graduate. He holds a bachelor's degree in English and a minor in psychology. He has published fiction and poetry in *Shale*, UK's campus literary magazine, and he has contributed to the campus newspaper. In his free time, he enjoys hiking, reading, and performing stand-up comedy.